THE MISSING ASTRA OF KRISHNA

THE MISSING ASTRA OF KRISHNA

Rajat K.

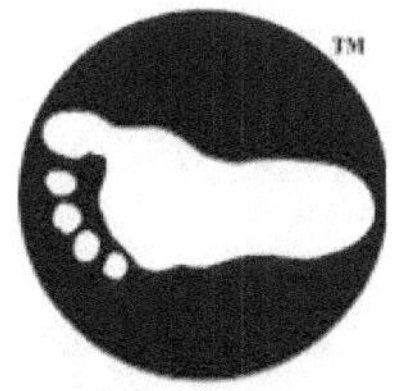

Bigfoot Publications

Because, there's a writer in everyone.

The Missing ASTRA of Krishna
Author : Rajat K.

First Published by
Bigfoot06 Publications (OPC) Pvt. Ltd.
1st floor, BSR Building near Vishal Mega Mart,
Daultabad Flyover, Laxman Vihar Phase 3,
Gurugram, Haryana (122001)
Website: www.bigfootpublications.in
Email: info@bigfootpublications.in

First Edition : November, 2023
© Rajat K.

ISBN Print Book - 978-81-19512-83-6

Typeset in Garamond 12pt
by Yachika Prajapati For Bigfoot06 Publications

Printed in India

Dedicated to my lovely wife, who has been an inspiration in every aspect of my life, and to my child, who I hope will one day see the world through her own eyes, shaped by my ideas.

About the author

Rajat K. grew up in a small township that takes pride in building the powerhouses of India, the Chittaranjan Locomotive Works. He graduated in Electronics and Communication Engineering from Asansol Engineering College and entered the corporate world. There, he has been associated with cutting-edge technology implementation and the lifeline of the nation, the telecommunications industry, for the last twenty years. He holds a Master's degree in Business Administration from IIT Kharagpur and later honed his skills through a Post Graduate Diploma in Data Science from IIIT Bangalore. He is based in Kolkata.

Since childhood, he has had a deep interest in mythologies, early human history, and the great epics of the land, which were regularly discussed and debated in his family.

He is married to Swagata, who is a scientist by qualification and a lecturer by profession. They share the same heart and mind when it comes to their dreams and passions. They are blessed with a beautiful daughter, Reneissa.

This book is his debut novel, and it represents an attempt to offer a fresh perspective on well-known and popular stories. His goal is to extract the meaning from ancient lore and bring hidden knowledge to light.

You can connect with Rajat K. through the following channels :

Facebook : *https://www.facebook.com/rajat.pramanik.5/*
Instagram : *https://www.instagram.com/pramanikrajat/*
Twitter : *https://twitter.com/rajat_pramanik*
LinkedIn : *https://www.linkedin.com/in/rajat-kumar-pramanik/*

Disclaimer

This is purely a work of fiction, enriched with facts that have surrounded us in our culture, tradition, and myths for centuries. These facts are drawn from different available, widely accepted, or speculated references. All attempts to recreate ideas are in correlation with the requirements of fictional narratives within the story, and are never intended to harm or disprove anyone or their beliefs.

Acknowledgements

To begin with, fiction is a work of imagination, but it requires some material facts as the building blocks upon which a story can be based. I am truly indebted to my parents who encouraged such ingenuity from my early childhood. Their knowledgeable insights and inspirations helped me understand the true meanings of the earliest histories of our lands through various versions and visions, often referred to as mythologies by many.

In addition, I owe gratitude to a true friend, my wife, who encouraged and supported me in putting my ideas into thoughtful and meaningful sentences, which ultimately formed the structure of this story. Without her tireless efforts in formatting, editing, and proofreading, along with invaluable suggestions, fact checks and eye for details, this composition might never have seen the light of day.

I am also thankful for my circle of selected friends who patiently listened to my jumbled concepts in the early days of conceiving the idea of writing this story.

One person who consistently provided me with collated information regarding my subject is a Doctor, a philosopher, and an expert in the eternal practices of truth, who also happens to be my Mother-in-Law by relation. She significantly assisted with the final proofreading and offered valuable comments for any modifications required in the context of the story.

Special thanks to Suparna Biswas for the beautiful illustrations to design the covers of this book, that provided stunning visuals and perception about the story.

I am grateful to the entire team at Bigfoot Publications who helped my ideas come to life in the form of this book. Special thanks to Deepak Yadav, who supported me as a true friend with his vast knowledge in the publishing industry, along with his marketing and promotional skills.

Last but not the least, as I did not adhere to the traditional form of creating a manuscript, it was the invaluable support from Microsoft Corporation, Alphabet Inc., and Steve Jobs without whom it would not have been possible for me to reach the printing press!

ॐ असतो मा सद्गमय ।
तमसो मा ज्योतिर्गमय ।
मृत्योर्मा अमृतं गमय ।
ॐ शान्तिः शान्तिः शान्तिः ॥

O Lord, Lead me to the Truth from Ignorance
Lead me to the Light from Darkness
Lead me to Immortality from the Death
Om Peace Peace Peace

जगन्नाथः स्वामी नयन पथ गामी भवतु मे ॥

O Jagannatha, Lord of the Universe, kindly be visible unto me

February, 3102 BC: Bhalka

The hunter cried inconsolably as he saw his Lord dying. He had never thought in his life that he would ever be able to see his Lord in person. And now, He was lying before him in a pool of blood.

The Lord blessed him and said, 'O Jara, don't be disheartened. For me, this is the path of salvation, as I have kept my word from our previous birth. There are dark times ahead. You have to undertake the responsibility of saving the future generations from the impending danger. You must take my belongings to Dwarka and hand them over to the greatest warrior of all. Only he can carry them to a safe place.'

Krishna smiled for the last time and proceeded to His heavenly abode.

Jara carried out his tasks as instructed by Krishna and returned to the temple, which was built by the Moon God Himself. He lived there and dedicated his life to the service of Lord Shiva. At times, he would share his experience with his fellow devotees and the knowledge he gained through that disastrous phase of his life.

x

December, 1025 AD
Somnath Temple

It was a cold and dark night. The whole kingdom was fast asleep, but the King was wide awake as he paced in his palace, filled with anxiety. Brisk gusts of chilly winds blowed over the kingdom. The heavy metallic window frames of his chamber were rattling. Beads of sweat trickled down his face, he could feel his heart pounding against his ribs.

King Bheemadeva walked into his private chamber to concentrate. He had already received the news that Mahmud was crossing Thar Desert and advancing towards his kingdom. He meticulously reviewed the series of events that had unfolded over the past few months.

King Debashalim and Paramdev had built up a fierce resistance against Mahmud with an army of forty thousand brave and well-trained soldiers. They were even assisted by the Ismaili Shias. These Ismailis from Sindh and Iran were Muslims who had fled and sought refuge in India after enduring torture and facing high Jizya taxes in their homeland. However, the Indian side of the army was no match for the horse-riding invaders led by the formidable Mahmud.

The King believed that his land was protected by the Supreme God Himself and guarded by His pious devotees who were ready to sacrifice their lives in the name of the Lord.

But he did not want bloodshed. Earlier in the day, an astrologer had come to his court and advised him to refrain from any kind of warfare for the next few days. Any offensive action by the King would cast a bad spell on the people of the land.

Bhima emerged from his chamber and ordered the High Priest to open the three main gates of the temple. The invader may have had the intention of looting the wealth preserved inside the temple but should spare the commoners if he encountered no resistance. Little did he know that this raid was more of a quest for wealth. The primary intention was to gain access to the original knowledge hidden in the temple, news of which had spread to distant lands beyond the westernmost boundaries. That knowledge, if luck permitted, would make one invincible in the physical world.

Contents

Chapter One

PRESENT DAY

It was a high-level boardroom meeting in the DRDO Office, commonly known as CHESS, in Hyderabad. Recent developments in international politics had created a new Axis. India, as a new superpower, had to choose a critical path to align itself with world politics.

Atomic warfare, once considered a prestigious and powerful arena, was now a thing of the past. The world had realized that it would annihilate the winning side as well. Who would risk such a strategy where the winner would have nothing to rule? Now, countries were preparing ways to defeat their enemies through strategically targeted strikes, strong enough to break the opponent's backbone and secure the resources of the ceded states.

The venue was selected to gather the best engineering minds in the fields of High Energy Weapons and Systems. Representatives from various DRDO departments were invited. Among them were scientists from Advanced Systems Laboratory (ASL) in Hyderabad, the Centre for High Energy Systems and Sciences (CHESS) in Hyderabad, and the Advanced Centre for Research in High Energy Materials (ACRHEM) in Hyderabad. Teams from Missile and Strategic Systems, such as the Defence Research & Development Laboratory (DRDL) in Hyderabad and the Research Centre Imarat (RCI) in Hyderabad, were also present. Researchers from Aeronautics and Avionics departments, including the Aeronautical Development Establishment (ADE) in Bengaluru, the Centre for Air Borne System (CABS) in Bengaluru, and the Defence Avionics Research Establishment (DARE) in Bengaluru, were in attendance. Members from Computational and Advanced Systems, including the Advanced Numerical Research & Analysis Group (ANURAG) in Hyderabad, and the Centre for Advanced Systems (CAS) in Hyderabad, were also part of the meeting.

The meeting was convened by representatives of the departments responsible for strengthening the Indian arsenal with High Precision weapons. Delegates from the Home Ministry, Ministry of Defence, and selected members from the Army, Air Force, and Navy were present. It was a week-long workshop where they would brainstorm new initiatives and strategies for the nation's future.

After a long and tiresome marathon discussion, it was decided that a multi-disciplinary team would be formed for research and development of advanced weapons that would bolster the Indian arsenal, providing strength and deterrence against world superpowers. The focus was on developing something with an indigenous concept, aligned with the vision of Make in India, and unique on the global stage.

The Director of DRDO, Dr. P. Krishnaswamy, turned on the projector as he concluded his welcome speech in the boardroom. He had prepared a very brief and pertinent presentation himself. Those present waited in anticipation.

The very first slide featured an image of Lord Krishna delivering great lessons to Arjuna just before the famous War at Kurukshetra. These lessons later became famous as Shrimad Bhagawat Geeta. Everyone knew that the Director was a devout follower of Lord Krishna, though not from a religious perspective. He always considered Lord Krishna the greatest Project Manager of all time. In many of his earlier lectures, he described how the Lord had exhibited all the standard frameworks of a Project with great excellence. It was obvious that he would begin such an important presentation with an image of Lord Krishna.

The second slide contained only three pictures. In the centre was an image of the infamous atomic blast at Hiroshima, with two smaller pictures, one of scientist Robert Oppenheimer on the left and another a depiction from the Geeta—the Virata form of Lord Krishna during His manifestation of the Universal form (Vishvarupa) before Arjuna. Dr. Krishnaswamy said, 'Dear all, this was the turning point of human civilization in the development of weapons of mass destruction. We all know how Oppenheimer realized his mistake after Project Trinity and said before the world those famous lines, "*Now I am become*

Death, the destroyer of worlds." Today in the twenty-first century, we must not do anything, for which we will not have any answer for future generations.'

The Director continued to the third slide, which displayed the magnificent indigenous Brahmos Missile. This was a scientific marvel, designed in collaboration with an ally and a source of national pride. Mass production of this precise and destructive weapon had secured the country's position in the international arena of warfare. Showing this slide, the Director conveyed a message about India's present military advancements and future prospects.

The last slide contained a picture of a woman holding a red apple on her head, with an archer aiming at the apple. A big red Question Mark appeared at the bottom. Dr. Krishnaswamy pointed out, 'Precision, my friends. Precision is the only thing we need. This project is all about precision. Research needs to be done to develop a weapon that can hit the target with the least collateral damage but inflict serious destruction. And now, the floor is all yours.' This was his famous way of concluding any presentation, creating a room for the audience to discuss, have an interactive session, express their opinions, and clear any doubts.

After several rounds of questions and answers, clarification of doubts, and brief discussions among the audience, the meeting adjourned for the day with an evening tea break.

The next day, a committee was formed to select representatives to create a team that would further brainstorm about the project. Their main task would be to design strategies and plans for further project development. Advaita Burman, a scientist from the High Energy Weapons department (CHESS) was made the Project Lead. He would primarily be assisted by Yogamaya Banerjee, also a scientist in Computational Systems, from the Advanced Numerical Research & Analysis Group (ANURAG). Other team members selected were scientists from various allied departments: Farah Choudhary from the Advanced Centre for Research in High Energy Materials (ACRHEM), Anjan Mathew from the Centre for Air Borne System (CABS), and Virat Sahni from Defence Avionics Research Establishment (DARE). Everyone wished them well for the success of their project.

The Last Days

Sudarshan was deeply saddened by the duty that had just been bestowed upon him by his Lord. He had nothing to do but obey the orders. Never in his life had he felt such anguish in his heart. He set off to behead His own bloodline as an instrument to bring an end to an era and completed the task as desired. But right after, for the first time since his birth, Sudarshan made his own choice. He did not return to his Master after this execution. Instead, he veered off on a journey far away towards the East and settled in an unknown place near the eastern seas. Krishna knew very well in His heart that it was the destiny of His most trusted companion. He just waited for an appropriate time to meet him again in the future. After ages, they met again. But this time, the Lord did not have His hand to hold Sudarshan upright. Neither was His companion in his earlier destructive form.

Jara secretly performed the last rites of the Lord. He arranged a pyre with whatever resources he could gather, laid his Lord on it, and *lit it. This was all he could do to facilitate his Lord's return to His heavenly abode. After some time, when the Lord had completely vanished through the fire, he observed a certain object still lying there in the pile of unburnt woods. He took it out and tried to hold it in his hand but felt that it was too heavy for him. He was perplexed and confused. Just then, he remembered the series of instructions that his Lord had given him on His deathbed. He somehow managed to build a boat out of those pyre woods and sailed in the seas, setting off on a long journey to carry that mysterious object to its designated place. Months and years passed. Finally, he could see the eastern shoreline. He left his boat in the middle of the sea and swam to reach the coast. Upon arrival, he placed the object deep within the earth in a dense forest, in the darkness of night, and then returned from whence he came. Nobody noticed this entire episode, and thus it lay there safely, hidden in the annals of time.*

The pyre woods floated in the sea for ages. When the appropriate time arrived, these woods would land on the shore.

THE TEAM

It was time for the group of selected scientists to form a team. Though everyone was under the umbrella of the same organization, it was not quite easy to know each other from different departments. That needed a personal interaction.

After a formal introduction of themselves before every other member, they decided to have a team lunch at a nearby restaurant. From now on, they would spend time together to develop, nurture and dedicate themselves fully towards shaping their ideas and thought processes.

Farah broke the ice. 'So, what will be the direction to our objective? Where should we start from?' she said.

She belonged to an affluent family with farming background in a small village near Lucknow, where education was not given much importance. People of her village, including her own family, were quite orthodox in following their particular faith. Many age-old customs and practises were still followed by them in verbatim, as was available in their holy text, and they did not bother to question the practicality of many actions dictated in their religion. From her childhood days, she had watched how the people of her community had laboured their whole life searching for a modest livelihood. But they lived in peace, and with simplicity. However, in such an odd surroundings, she was fortunate enough to be born in a family where moral values and personal bonding prevailed. She was the youngest of her five siblings, and was quite pampered by her parents. Also, she always had her grandmother by her side. Her grandmother had a tremendous influence on her life. Though it was quite uncommon, she would often narrate various different stories, including those from other religious beliefs. She depicted the incidents from those chapters to her granddaughter and instilled a belief in her that they were not mere mythologies, but histories which had been in oblivion for great lengths of time. As people did not see those in their own eyes and did not have the capacity to understand many scientific facts embedded in those stories, gradually the history turned into myth. Her descriptions made those episodes as vivid and lively as if they were from some recent past. It was from this that Farah had developed a great interest in the two great epics of our land. By nature, she was smart, logical, outspoken and was quite of a garrulous type.

As the Project Lead, it was Advaita's turn for an answer and pave the path for the future course of action. He belonged to a town in North Bengal, named Cooch Behar. People of this place had a great pride for themselves. The town was dotted with beautiful architectural buildings and temple structures. Among them, the most famous of all was the Royal Palace of Coochbehar, which was a replica of the world-famous British Royal Palace, the Buckingham Palace of London. The place was also famous for another reason. The Princess of the Royal family was married to the Prince of Jaipur. Thus, in spite of being situated in one eastern corner, it was the centre of discussion all over the country. His family hailed education as the ultimate tool for success in life. Priority was always given to livelihood over life. Naturally, he was brought up with a sense of being a successful bread-owner in the family. Though he often had doubts over his family's beliefs, he never protested them as he had no other alternative independent perspective in life then. He always dreamt of tearing the family shackles and living life in his own way once he would become so-called successful, as defined by his parents. But he knew that he would have to wait for that perfect time, place and condition to happen.

'In my opinion,' he replied, 'our research objective will be to develop a weapon of war with the highest precision, the Director has made THIS very clear. It must be capable of hitting the target, and should be re-usable.' He reminded how the Director had emphasized that funding for weapons development would create a huge hole in the national exchequer. He continued, 'All the advanced countries are now researching on reusable weapons, or at least the multi-stage carriers. Our former President, the great Sir A. P. J. Abdul Kalam, also dreamt of reusable Brahmos missiles. So, we must think of something that is of high precision and re-usable in nature.'

Yogamaya raised her hand, and Advaita nodded without looking into her eyes. Adding some more points to the discussion, she said, 'We must concentrate on Robotics and Artificial Intelligence as our guiding mantra. It will destroy our enemy, but it must not be the object of hatred and fear as a lethal weapon of mass-destruction. We must incorporate some humane qualities to this as this must be capable of sparing the innocent people, and thus will be an instrument of protection for the good.'

Yogamaya belonged to a family of medical background from Central Kolkata. She grew up seeing her parents to be always busy with patients the whole day at hospitals and medical centres. She patiently waited for their return in the evening to spend some time together, but was often disappointed. Her father was of a very practical nature, and inspired her to build a successful career to be prosperous in life, while her mother was of a very exceptional nature. She would spend her whole day inculcating the cutting-edge advancements of science in the medical world. In the evening, she would retire and delve deep in spiritual world. She always made it a point to devote some of her time from her daily busy schedule towards some traditional religious activities. She was very much pious from her heart. Yogamaya would often help her mother perform Pujas in their house on many an occasions. She would listen to her mother describing the necessity and benefits of such rituals in daily life. It was from her mother that she imbibed the interest to know about the old and so-called obsolete scriptures of the past. Her mother would always help her understand the meanings of those scriptures in a very lucid way, and that made her a vivid reader of those old scriptures from an early age. Though it was a perfect family and people of her neighbourhood would often envy them, she sometimes felt loneliness from the bottom of her heart. She often felt it difficult to share many casual and frivolous talks that a girl of her age would do in the family.

It was Anjan's turn to add something. He came from Bangalore, and his father was a Wing Commander in the Indian Air Force. His father was a devout follower, and he accompanied his family every weekend to the local prayer halls. Along with all other people assembled there, he praised the power and benevolence of the Almighty. He loved listening to particular verses from the gospels where descriptions of ancient flying vehicles and personal interaction of earlier priests with the messengers of God were read out. In his childhood, he always loved playing with remote-controlled toy aeroplanes and helicopters, and dreamt of flying those actual gorgeous machines himself one day. Though he always dreamt of becoming a heroic fighter jet pilot just like his father, his dreams could not be fulfilled because of his poor eyesight. Then he made up his mind to become someone who would be closely associated with these marvellous flying objects. It was because of his passion that he became a scientist in avionics.

Anjan added, 'This must be a flying machine capable of high range flights, maybe like our Intercontinental Ballistic Missiles. We can develop some carrier to fly long distances. But how can it be so accurate to hit only a precision target, small enough not to create any collateral damage! This may be a major point in our research.'

Only Virat was left. He said, 'That is where we need to work upon. It must be designed so that it can be controlled even when it is at a great distance. The guiding system should have minimum latency to manoeuvre it if the target changes its location swiftly.'

Virat's father was a professor of history at Delhi University. He was very close to his father, and he naturally developed an interest in national and international chronicles. He held the popular belief that histories were stories written to glorify the ruling authorities. He would often discuss at length with his father regarding various historical topics of controversy. Their favourite topic of brainstorming was the Aryan invasion theory, which has been nullified by many modern historians, based on scientific studies and with the help of genetic mapping of different groups of people, both from the indigenous population as well from those living in the central Asian regions. His father used to tell him that history was not only written in the pages of the books, but are available in plain sight in the midst of the current living people who are carrying those stories of the past. One can learn a lot about the past generations simply by listening to the common folklores that are practised and memorised. Also, history is available in the rocks, in the inscriptions, and in the architectural remains which have survived the tests of time.

The team discussed and tried to figure out many other points. But, Advaita felt that it was going quite too long. One thing he noticed was that every team member had a deep root of understanding of culture of India, and every one of them took great interest in the myths and available advanced concepts that were hidden there. But, it was quite tough to decide on the prototype on the very first day of discussion.

There was a large OLED television set placed on one of the walls of the restaurant, opposite to the table where they were sitting. Everyone was periodically looking at that. A movie of the famous Predator series was playing there. In one of the scenes, the leader of the humungous monsters was throwing a saucer-like weapon at the enemies.

It would slice the throats of the enemies, or would create a blast of devastating impact, and always returned to the monster to throw it again.

Suddenly the idea of the prototype clicked in their mind. Four things were happening before their eyes – highly destructive, high precision, working at the command of the user, and returning for re-use. They knew what they were looking for.

The group cheered in unison – the SUDARSHAN CHAKRA!!!

The team sighed in relief as they looked at each other. They could not believe themselves. How could they not comprehend such an obvious answer. They felt a new energy and passion flowing inside them. Everyone hugged each other. But Advaita softly touched Yogamaya's hand. It was time for them to retire to their respective guest houses. They decided to meet at Advaita's Office the next day.

The King

Indradyumna was keeping himself abreast of all the proceedings which were happening around Hastinapur. He was intentionally keeping himself away. After all, the two former kings from that kingdom, Vinda and Anuvinda, took part alongside the lines of the Kauravas in the Great War. He was hesitant to make direct contact with the present Chakravarty Emperor Yudhisthira.

Avanti was a prosperous land. The borders of the kingdom stretched from the north to the south of Aryavarta. The land was split into two halves by the mighty Vetravati river. The southern part was ruled by his ally from Mahismati, while, he himself controlled the northern part from his capital at Ujjaini.

Indradyumna was a pious king, having attained the title of the 'King of the Sages', a Rajarshi, and was a great devotee of Lord

Vishnu. He often arranged debates and discussions regarding various religious topics in his court. On one such occasion, there arrived a great sage who had roamed all around the earth. The sage proudly described that he had visited the most sacred pilgrimage of the Lord in the whole world. On further inquisition from the King, he narrated his experience at the auspicious land of Woodra Desha, where local tribal people were worshipping a magnificent blue stone they had unearthed from the forest sometime back. People were venerating their respect to this blue stone as Lord Neelmadhav. The locals believed that this was a part of the Lord Himself, and so the Lord was actually residing there. On hearing the narration in details, the King immediately recognized that blue stone, and remembered his duty towards protecting the Lord. He planned his next course of action without wasting any further time.

Chapter Three

TRAVEL TO SOMNATH

It was a new day and the team was all geared up. They were all reminiscing the discussion of the earlier day. Everyone was thrilled. Quite naturally, the team became friends and started calling each other with their pet names.

Adi began, 'So, we all have to pursue what we have decided yesterday. Now let's make a plan to achieve it.' He looked carefully at all the team members, and tried to fathom what was going on in their minds.

'I have heard a lot about this from my Dadi,' Farah said. 'She had a great interest in this, and told stories of how the weapon was acquired by Vishnu, and how he used it. I always dreamt of finding this some other day, when I grow up. And now, I am into this project of making a prototype of this!' She exclaimed as the sheer thought of discovering the most venerated weapon of all time flashed in her eyes.

Virat said, 'I think we should start from where it all ended.' He looked at others, as they were curious of what he meant. He tried to explain in details, as he continued 'I mean, we should begin our research from ground zero. We all know, it is believed, that the Chakra went within the earth at the place where Krishna left his mortal body and proceeded to Baikuntha. The place where Krishna died is believed to be in a forest at a place called Bhalka. The place must have a great significance and might give us some clue.'

Everyone nodded, expecting to explore more about the place. Maya added, 'Also, some conspiracy theory says that it was transported to the nearby Somnath temple and was placed under the Shivalinga. People believed that the weapon had a divine power even after Krishna left it after His death. That, they say, was the mystery behind the levitating Shivalinga at the temple.'

Anjan did not say much. He was thrilled from his heart imagining the adventures that lay ahead in pursuit of the technology to build such a weapon.

The team planned their itinerary based on their discussions. Except Anjan, all four of them were already acquainted with various myths and folklores related to Puranas from their childhood. They decided to study and research extensively on the background and stories associated with the places where they had planned to visit. This would facilitate them to develop ideas and adopt inspirations for their project.

The Somnath temple, also called Deo Patan, was one of the most sacred pilgrimage sites for the Hindus. It is situated in Prabhas Patan, Veraval in the state of Gujarat. The temple was believed to house the first among the twelve Jyotirlinga shrines of Lord Shiva.

Bhalka was just four kilometres away from Prabhas Patan. The majority of the mainstream people believed that Lord Krishna died near Somnath, not knowing the exact location. But, only a few knew that it was Bhalka where Krishna died. There were also footprints available at that place. Later, a magnificent temple was built in commemoration of Lord Krishna there.

There were many routes to reach Somnath. One could take a flight to Surat Airport, and then a road journey which required almost over thirteen and a half hours of travel time. It was also reachable from Ahmedabad Airport, by road that took over twelve and a half hours. But the majority of the tourists reached Rajkot Airport, and then took a road trip to reach there in six and a half hours. However, the nearest Airport was Diu Airport, from where one could reach Somnath in only an hour or so.

They decided to choose the last option. Everyone took a leave as they had to pack their belongings and check out from their guest houses in Hyderabad. A chartered plane was arranged for a late afternoon flight that would take them to Diu.

Everything was planned earlier. A middle-aged man was waiting for them at the Diu Airport exit gate. He handed Adi the key of a car, which was waiting at the parking. He thanked the man and the group proceeded towards the parking lobby.

Adi handed over the key to Anjan. Besides being passionate about his remote-controlled toys from childhood, Anjan also harboured a great interest and passion for driving cars. In their earlier discussions, Anjan had described how he would often venture into long drives after stealing the keys of his father's car, while his father was away, and roamed around the small hills near Bengaluru. Adi remembered this. Though he was the most shy person among the group, the responsibility of driving for the next few days could reliably be handed over to him.

Anjan took to the wheels, while Adi took the front left seat of the spacious vehicle. This was an apt and comfortable car for their next few days of adventure. The other three took their seats in the middle. The last rows of seats were folded to accommodate their luggage in the boot.

While entering the car, Adi faced a little difficulty in opening the left front door. A black Audi Q7 was parked at an angle beside their car. It was as if the car was parked in a hurry, and the driver did not notice that it might cause problem for the other car. Adi frowned, but did not give any importance to this as this might happen to anyone.

Somnath temple square was about sixty-three kilometres away from Diu Airport. The road was quite good, and the team did not face any difficulty in reaching their hotel, which was just half a kilometre away from the main temple complex. They checked in their rooms, and decided to have an early dinner so that they could start the next day timely.

Following a sumptuous dinner in the luxurious hotel lounge, they all bid good night to each other.

Adi went to bed and started seeing some documents and whereabouts regarding their project topic. He always had a habit of reading some books in bed, as that helped him to have a good sleep.

The hotel telephone, kept at the bedside, rang. It was quite unexpected at such a late hour of the night, as there was nothing ordered from the room service, and they had completed all formalities at the reception during their check-in. He picked up the receiver in anticipation, and there was Maya on the other side of the line. She apologized for calling him up so late, and asked for a paracetamol. She was having a throbbing headache. 'Do you have something to ease my pain?', asked Maya. Adi always carried some basic medicines like paracetamol, a combination of Ornidazole and Ofloxacin, some antibiotics and a few more, during all his trips as a precautionary first aid measure. He sensed her discomfort and assured her that he would bring some paracetamol without any delay.

Chapter Four

SOMNATH VISIT

It was a coincidence that Adi's and Maya's hotel rooms were adjacent. He knocked at the door, the door was unlocked from within, it opened slowly.

Adi entered the room, holding a strip of paracetamol in his hand. All the lights in the room were switched off, except the bedside lamp. He felt quite nervous. Maya was sitting on the bed, crouching her head with her palms. Adi offered the medicine, and took a bottle to pour some water. As he held the medicine towards her, she stretched her hand. Their fingers touched. It was a familiar touch, and he felt a shivering flowing down his spine. It was almost ages that he had gotten her touch. He softly looked into her face, into her eyes. That compassionate smile, those familiar lips were too enticing to resist. He held her in his arms. He kissed her on her forehead, on her nose, then on her cheeks. He lowered his mouth and deeply kissed her on her lips. She reciprocated warmly. The two lovers have been longing for one another for years now. They terribly missed each other. Miles of separation, years of detachment vanished into a puff. There was no awkwardness, no inhibition. The night stood still, moments froze, a tsunami of feelings swept them away. They passionately made love.

They were batchmates in IIT Kharagpur, and were best of friends. She was from a big city, while he was a small town boy. As opposites would attract, their friendship turned into something very special. They often bunked their classes mutually, and would sit by the technology stadium and spend hours together. Adi did not use to talk much, as he was a good listener. It was Maya who always kept the conversation alive. She had now got someone to hear all her thoughts, which she always longed. On the weekends, they would roam around the technology market, and would give a try for some movies in the technology auditorium. Years passed, and their bond became stronger. It was in the seventh semester when they realised their true love for each other. But, that was the time to fully concentrate on the curriculum and prepare themselves for the ensuing campus interviews and selections. They broke the norm, and both decided not to appear for the campus interview process. They both were very meritorious students, and wished to get higher education before walking into the corporate world. Adi got admission in M. Tech at IIT Delhi, and Maya went to MIT, Cambridge. Though both were happy as their career progressed, they realized that their days of togetherness were numbered. They promised to stay in touch with each other. Days turned into months, and months turned into years. Their long distance relationship started becoming strenuous and difficult to maintain. They both tried hard, but slowly and steadily their connections faded. They became so busy during their research days that there was hardly any communication with each other. Finally, their relationship was buried in time.

But fate had planned something else for them. They again both joined in DRDO, but at different departments, at different locations. They were unaware of the fact of their engagement in the same institute. It was only during the workshop in the last week that they saw each other, when their old memories kindled once again. And now, they were in the same team.

They both shared their past years sitting on the bed. How they missed each other so badly during the initial phase, and how they gradually coped with their emotions and diverted their attention to higher studies and research work. They had vowed not to be in any relationship any more. And now, they were together. They felt refreshed and relived. Her headache had long gone.

The night was unusually quiet, quite contrary to the upsurge in feelings they had locked inside, waiting to be vented out. But now they had grown up, and were professionals. It was quite late. It was time to leave. Next day was crucial. Adi kissed her again, and bid her goodnight. He returned to his room, and both had a good night's sleep.

The next morning they all met at the breakfast table. Farah proposed that they should start from Dwarka, the land of Lord Krishna. She had also made an itinerary for the next two days. First, they could go to Dwarkadheesh

Temple, then to Okha port to reach Bhet Dwarka by ferry, which was thirty-five kms away. They could also visit Gomti river, Rukmini Temple, Sudama temple, and Porbandar. There was also a light and sound show at Junagarh fort in the evening to enjoy, where the life and different incidents related to Lord Krishna were shown. Nageshwar Temple, another one of the twelve jyotirlingas, was only eighteen kilometres from Dwarka. This city was a perfect place for one to enrich both spiritual excellence and soak in the beautiful Arabian Sea for rejuvenation. They could also visit Gir forest that was just thirty-seven kilometres from Somnath, and enjoy a jungle safari.

Virat insisted that though Dwarka was a good choice, as a major portion of life of the Lord was spent there, but the real mystery was in the Somnath temple. So they must concentrate there.

Everyone agreed to start with Somnath Temple. It was just a walking distance to the temple compound from their hotel.

They were sitting on the grass in the temple compound that was soaked in dew. Other visitors were queueing up to get inside the temple, which opened at 6:00 in the morning. The team had reached there just after the morning *Aarti* (prayer) performed at 8:00 am. There were two more *Aarti* timings, one at 12:00 noon and another at 7:00 pm in the evening after which the temple was closed sharp at 8:00 pm.

The temple premises was large. Built with sandstone, the *shikhara* (dome) of the temple was fifteen metres in height, with a flag post of over eight metres tall on the top. It was quite a long process to enter the temple. Being a high-security area, visitors were screened and frisked twice before entering the main building. Visitors were not allowed to carry any electronic items including mobiles, cameras or even car keys. Also, any type of leather items like belts or purses were not allowed. There was provision of lockers for safekeeping of the restricted items.

The team decided that they would attend the special *Aarti* at 12:00 noon. As they entered the temple complex, they were spellbound by the superb architecture of the temple. The whole temple was built in Chalukya style architecture. It was magnificent and awe-inspiring. They attended the prayers with deep devotion. They however did not enter the sanctum sanctorum as touching the Shivalinga was not allowed, as it was one of the *Jyotirlingas* (radiant Sign of Lord Shiva). They felt a positive vibe and energy flowing inside them.

It was an invigorating experience for all them, as they decided to spend some more time in the premises.

Woodra Desha

Indradyumna called for his chief priest and requested him to discover the sacred place, as narrated by the great sage. Vidyapati set out to Woodra Desha alone in search of Neelmadhav. But luck was not in his favour. He roamed around in the forest for days, trying to figure out each and every clue as described in the royal court, but could not decide where to search from, or how to get the whereabouts of Neelmadhav. He roamed around the place without food and shelter. One day, while he was very tired and thirsty, he lost his consciousness in the deep jungle. When he woke up, he found himself lying inside an elegant hut, surrounded by some people with peculiar dresses made from natural fibres, barks of trees and animal hides, with long headgears and spears in their hands. One of them, a well-built man, standing taller than the rest, was greeted with respect by some guards. He was wearing beautiful heavy necklaces made from sea-shells, and was adorned with a fresh peacock feather on his special headgear. Vidyapati quickly understood that he was among the local tribal people, and the man in front of him was their chief. One thing that made him relieved in these odd surroundings was that he had at last been able to find the local tribesmen as per the depiction. The leader of the group introduced himself as Viswavasu. He assured him of safety and described how his fellowmen had brought him to this place while he was lying in a helpless state in the forest. He asked him to stay there till he felt himself fit enough to return to his homeland.

Lalita was personally taking care of this foreign man. She had never seen such a fair complexioned man within her tribe or in her known territory. She naturally felt attracted to this young man, who often told him stories of the world about which she always dreamt of. On the other hand, the girl told him stories of her tribe, the deeds of her father as the chief of the Savaras, and their custom of worshipping the living God Neelmadhav. Soon they both fell in love with each other, and decided to marry. Though it was against the custom to be engaged in a nuptial bond with anyone outside of the tribe, Viswavasu agreed on the marriage between his daughter and Vidyapati.

As per the Savara rituals, it was a practice for the newly-weds to take blessings from the living God. Vidyapati could not believe he was finally going to succeed in his mission. But he was again dismayed when two of Viswavasu's aides blindfolded him, and the couple were led to a cave on that new-moon night where the God was worshipped. Vidyapati, as a last resort, made out a plan and took some mustard seeds and hid them in the folds of his palm. While they were returning from the cave, he quietly kept spreading the seeds on the soil.

Chapter Five

THE MYTH

The team continued discussing the myths associated with the temple, and also the recorded history available about it.

'As per popular beliefs, the temple was built by the Moon God Somraj with gold in the *Satyayuga*, as a token of appreciation to Lord Shiva, after He recovered from His sickness due to a curse from His own father-in-law', Farah started describing the background of Somnath temple. 'In *Tretayuga*, it was built by the infamous and most powerful Sri Lankan King Ravana, who was a great devotee of Shiva. It was rebuilt by Lord Krishna himself in *Dwaparyuga* with wood. In *Kaliyuga*, King Bhimdeva Solanki built it in stone.'

'The name of this place was mentioned in ancient scriptures as well, where it was named as *Prabhas Patan*. This was a place for pilgrimage as this was considered as a *Prayag* or *Triveni Sangam* in earlier days, where the mythological river Saraswati met with Hiranya and Kapila rivers'.

Farah continued, 'Around 649 AD, the dilapidated temple from the pre-Christian era was rebuilt by the Maitraka kings of Vallabhi. This structure was destroyed by Junayad, an Arab Governor of Sind, in 725 AD. This was the first attack and an act of Islamic barbarism on the temple'.

'King Nagabhatta II of the Gurjara-Pratihara dynasty reconstructed the temple around 815 AD. It was again beautified by the king of Solanki Dynasty, around 997 AD. This was the permanent structure that faced the wrath of the Muslim invaders several times, till the British took over the country in the eighteenth Century. Each time the temple was destroyed, it was rebuilt by devotees and kings to bring back the lost glory'.

Adi and Anjan thanked Farah for the detailed information. However, Virat wanted to add more to it. 'On January 6, 1026, Mahmud Ghazni attacked the temple, looted huge amounts of wealth, broke the ShivaLinga into pieces, and carried it back to be used on the steps of the Ghazni Mosque', he recounted as if he was visualizing the events. 'Hundreds of other idols were also destroyed and were used to construct the steps to the entrance of the Jama Masjid. It is said that he attacked the temple seventeen times. Each time that he attacked India, he made sure that he destroyed the temple and looted wealth from there. The temple was however rebuilt as a temporary wooden structure around 1027-1042 AD by King Bhoj of Paramara dynasty from Malwa and King Bhima of Solanki dynasty from Anhilwara. This wooden structure was later re-constructed in stone by King Kumarapala around 1150 AD'.

'In 1296 AD, about 275 years after Mahmud of Ghazni's attack, Allauddin Khilji destroyed the temple. In 1308 AD, King Mahipala I of Chudasama dynasty from Saurashtra rebuilt the temple. His son Khengar installed the Shivalinga inside the temple around 1340 AD'.

'Around 1395 AD, the temple was again attacked by Muzaffar Shah I from the Gujarat Sultanate. However, the temple was re-built by unknown devotees'.

Virat continued with a raze in his eyes, 'In 1706 AD, the Mughal Emperor Aurangzeb plundered the temple for one last time. It was said that he even paraded with the severed heads of hundreds of Hindu devotees in order to create terror and expel all the idol worshippers from the temple. After this attack, the temple was razed to the ground. The temple was reconstructed in 1783 AD at an adjacent site by Queen Ahilyabai Holkar of Indore, in co-operation with Chhatrapati Bhonsle of Kolhapur, the Peshwa of Pune, Raja Bhonsle of Nagpur, and Srimant Patilbuwa Shinde of Gwalior'.

'In 1947, the Iron Man of India, Sardar Ballav Bhai Patel reached Junagadh in order to consolidate the princely state with Gujarat, after the Nawab escaped to Pakistan', Virat took pride while retelling the accounts. 'He was traumatized by the dilapidated state of the temple, and took an oath that he would rebuild the temple and bring back the old splendour. It was under his patronage that the present day temple structure was finally completed by renowned architect Prabhaschandar in 1951. Dr. Rajendra Prasad, the first President of India, inaugurated the temple on 11th May of the same year, by installing the Shivalinga, and dedicated it to the citizen of the country'.

'Somnath temple was always the centre of attraction for the Muslim invaders', now Adi added on. 'But was it only for wealth or to create fear among the non-Muslims? People believed that the real motive was something else than that. Many ancient knowledge were accumulated in the temple. It was because of that that they repeatedly destroyed the temple, in the same way, that they destroyed other centres of knowledge, like the destruction of Taxila and Nalanda University'.

'Another theory was that the Muslims of early Iran and Persian area believed that Somnath (called '*Sumanat*' in Persian literature) was also a place of worship for Manat – one of the pre-Islamic Arab Goddesses. She was the elder sister of Al-Lat and Al-Uzza, and the trio was worshipped together in line with Hindu similarities of the Goddesses Mahashakti, Maha Lakshmi and Maha Saraswati. She was considered as a Goddess of fate, fortune, time and destiny. The attacks were not only symbols of conquest and victories, but were also symbols of fanatical intolerance and persecution. The plunders of the temple, with the killing of infidels were considered as a symbol of the revival of the Iranian identity boosted by religious zeal. The destruction of both Hindu Somnath temple and Manat was portrayed as an event for celebration'.

Fig. 1 : *2nd century AD relief from Hatra depicting the goddess al-Lat flanked by two female figures, possibly al-Uzza and Manat*

Fig. 2 : *'Eye' image often associated with these goddess*
(source : Wikipedia, Manat (goddess)
https://en.wikipedia.org/wiki/Manat_%28goddess%29)

Adi informed, 'There was a unique feature associated with the temple. It was built in such a place that if one looked southwards from the temple, there was no landmass till the South Pole. This was inscribed on the original *Baan Stambha,* a pillar constructed with an arrow-head atop, which was erected with the temple since the 7th Century AD. The people of this place were well aware of the world map long before the birth of modern cartography, and that again showed the wealth of knowledge that was available there'.

Fig. 3 : *Baan Stambha atop Somnath temple;*

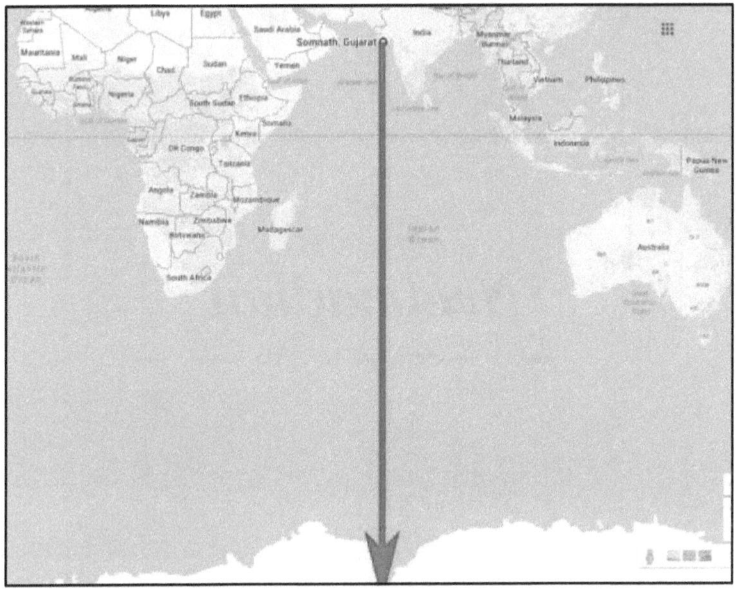

Fig. 4 : *Somnath to Antarctica, straight line without land (source: https://www.booksfact.com/history/somnath-antarctica-straight-line-without-land.html*

Maya concluded, 'The ancient inhabitants of these lands were sea-faring people, as is evident from many references in the *Vedas* and the *Puranas*. In fact, South pole and Antarctica are also mentioned in *Uttara Rayamana*, long back. Not only this, but there were also descriptions of the seven large islands including South America, the Polynesia and Australia, which were referred to as *Patala*, and ruled by our very indigenous rulers. But that is a different story to tell.'

Neelmadhav

Vidyapati returned to Avanti. He shared all his experiences with Indradyumna, the King. On hearing his account, the King was mesmerized. 'Are you sure of this ?', the King asked Vidyapati. Vidyapati nodded. The King knew what to do. He immediately drew plans to explore the divine place. He set out on a journey to the mentioned Sri Khetra in order to confirm the location of Neelmadhav. He was accompanied by a large contingent of his citizens and their families, who were willing to experience the Divine being. It was a long, tiresome journey. They arrived at nightfall. Exhausted from this strenuous travel, the King ordered them to set camps for the night. However, the King could not sleep. He was anxious. At midnight, he set out alone for the cave, following the trails created by Vidyapati. The blurred light from the crescent moon above the horizon was not enough to see through the dense forest. But by then, the seeds were full-grown mustard plants with full bloom, and their yellow hue was the pathfinder for the brave king.

He entered the cave, only to find it empty. Disheartened, the King sat down on the cold floor. 'The Lord does not want to be found', he thought in despair. He could feel his tears rolling down. The King rose with a heavy heart when he heard someone calling him by his name. Surprised, he saw the chief of the Savara tribe, Viswavasu, standing behind him. He greeted the King and expressed his relief, for someone who had the power to protect God's most precious thing had finally arrived. The Chief however asked for a guarantee of the safety and prosperity of his whole tribe on the land, for times to come.

On seeing the stone, which was covered in a black cloth, untouched by bare hands, the King realized that this was no ordinary object. He comprehended the adverse impact of the object if it was mishandled. He secretly hid that in sand under the temporarily built stables, where the horses of his army were being kept. He knew that anyone who would come in direct contact with the object would unknowingly risk his own life. So he kept it away from the common people.

On the next morning, people were disheartened to know that Lord Neelmadhav had disappeared from there. The King consoled them by swearing to build the most beautiful and magnificent temple in memory of the Lord that would instil awe, faith and reverence in common men for generations to come. He also described how he met the Lord in his dreams on the previous night. 'I promise you all, O great devotees and followers of the Lord, that this place will become His abode on earth. I also swear to perform a Sahasra Ashwamedha Yagna to please the Lord, in the meantime, during which this temple will be built. You all will love to call Him Lord Jagannatha.' Nobody noticed the grief in his eyes. They all hailed the King and patiently waited for the grand temple to be completed.

Chapter Six

UNEXPECTED DISCOVERY

After their prayers were over, they came out of the temple and decided to take a short tour of the Veraval city and its adjoining areas. While collecting their items from the locker, Adi noticed an old door just behind the security check post. It was locked and fenced off. On enquiry, the security guard at the frisking counter said that it was an underground passageway for the chief priest which was used in earlier days as an alternate route in times of emergency. Presently, no one was allowed to enter that passage.

Adi was excited to explore. But there was no permission to enter. Virat came up with an idea. He scribbled on a small chit of paper and handed over to a serviceman of the temple. After a short wait, a priest showed up. He was one of the high-ranking priests, presently serving as the Head of the steering committee in the temple. Virat immediately bowed down to touch his feet. The priest smiled and enquired about his father.

Years had passed since he met Virat's father, his old friend. During one of his earlier visits to the temple, the priest had promised him of a guided tour of the entire temple premises with special references to some old architectural relics which were oblivion to the eyes of a common visitor. But as his father was engaged in research and college responsibilities, he could never make time for a personal entourage. Last night, when Virat conversed with his father to brief him about his short expedition, his father remembered the days he spent in Somnath. He asked Virat to contact with his friend to acquire hidden information and deeper knowledge about the temple.

Virat introduced him to his team members, and requested him to take them to the restricted passageway. The priest nodded his head in disapproval. He said, 'I will not be able to co-operate with you as no one is officially permitted to enter'. Adi and Maya now approached and requested to allow them for once. After much pleading, the priest agreed. He told them to wait for some time. 'Come, it is time for a change of shift of the security personnel. During this transition, you can cross the fence without anyone noticing'. Pointing at Virat, he added, 'I am helping you on condition of anonymity. Promise me that no one must know about this. Your father is a good friend of mine, and a man of virtue. You must be truthful to your promise.'

The security at the check post repeatedly checked his leather strapped wrist watch. He was getting ready to leave. He left his register and pen on the small kiosk. As he bent down to collect his bag, he did not notice five people sneaking stealthily through the fence. As they stepped inside, the priest closed the door slowly behind them, locked it from outside and left.

It was quite dark in the passage, as they strained their eyes inside the chamber. Maya heard a soft thud but could not see anything. The light behind them had vanished. Anjan took out a torch from his waist pouch, and they moved forward. Maya screamed, 'Where is he? He was right behind.' Everyone turned around to notice. The heavy door was closed. The priest was nowhere to be seen. Anjan brought the torch to examine the entrance. The door was bolted from outside. Adi and Virat tried to slide the door open. It won't move an inch. Farah suggested, 'The only way is to move forward'.

It was damp inside, and it appeared indeed that no one entered there for a long time. There was a long stairway in front of them. They took to the stairs that led them one level below, and they reached a large hall at the end of it. There were rows of small rooms on three sides of the hall. Most of the rooms were closed with wooden doors and locked with wooden batons. On each of the two batons, a beautiful serpent design was crafted in such a fashion that when one locked the doors, the serpents made an inter-coiling design. Adi opened one of the doors and entered. There was a stone slab of about six feet long, with another elevated stone slab as head rest. There was some soot on a wall, possibly from an oil lamp.

On examining the carbon deposited on one of the walls, Farah said, 'It looks like old Buddhist quarters. The monks used to live here. The soot indicates that they used to read scriptures inside these rooms. The hall must be used as an assembly place during prayers.' They came out of the room and continued to explore. On the fourth wall of the hall where there were no such rooms, there was a large door with intricate wooden carvings. They pushed the heavy door to see another staircase leading downwards. The steps of the stairs were quite steep, as if to hinder someone for daily use. Also, there were no guard-rails for support. They carefully stepped down the stairs and reached another level below.

They reached an empty hall. The light from the pocket torch was not enough to illuminate the darkness. They waited for a moment to adjust their eyes in the dark. There were strange inscriptions all over the walls and on the roofs. As they trained their eyes, they were able to recognise some of the carvings depicting the life of Jataka. Those were the stories of Buddha from His earlier lives. Farah nodded as her assumption of Buddhist links with this underground chambers became evident. As they approached forward, they noticed that the two side walls of the hall were built at an angle which was gradually making the passage narrow. The passage ended at a wall of only about three feet wide. The wall in front of them had the head of the Buddha inscribed on it. This was quite unusual, as it was a practise inside such Buddhist monasteries to build a statue of Buddha in its full form. There was a halo carved behind the head. There was something uncommon with the halo. On closer examination, it appeared that the halo had intricately carved serrated edges on two layers, emanating from the centre and pointing outwards. The head was at the centre of it. From behind the head, flat spoke like carvings reached till the edges of the circumference, which gave it the appearance of a rotating wheel. They noticed that there were eight ruby stones attached just inside the circumference, at an angle of forty-five degrees from each previous one. Rubies were considered to attract solar energy. What was the purpose of attaching rubies to such a carving? What was it trying to indicate?

Anjan directed his torch to the left. There was a small passage perpendicular to the wall with this special carving. They expected to explore something more. But this time the passage came to a dead end. There was no opening on the wall as it was with the upper level. Just then a scary thought sank inside Maya's head, 'How do we get out of here?'. She felt the air heavy and was gradually finding it difficult to breathe. The stairs that led them to this second level were too slippery, steep and narrow. It was quite impossible to climb up to the first level. Even if they succeeded in reaching there, the heavy wooden door through which they entered the chamber was locked from the outside.

They started to pace up and down the hallway in search of an exit. At the junction of the dead-end and the perpendicular passage, right below the carving of the head, Virat noticed some drawings on the floor. On a closer inspection, it appeared that the drawing was the same as that on the wall of the carving. There was a thick layer of dust on the floor. Adi thought of something and grabbed the key of the car hanging out of Anjan's trousers. He began scraping the drawing with the key. The scraping revealed an exquisite disc, an exact replica of the halo. The eight sockets, where rubies were engraved earlier, were however empty. He examined the grooves closely and said, 'There may be an opening under this disc. These grooves might help us rotate the disc. Let's give it a try.' All of them started trying to rotate the disc in unison. There were altogether eight sockets. But the disc did not rotate a millimetre. Virat said thoughtfully, 'If we have to rotate the disc in order to find a passage, then there must be a key to open it. How do we open a lock? We need to match the grooves of a key with that of a lock. Right?' Everyone understood what he was trying to indicate. Now the four of them put their hands on alternate sockets, while Anjan pointed his torch on the floor. Surprisingly, while they were not able to rotate the disc by putting their hands on consecutive sockets, this time the disc showed some indication of movement. They tried hard to match four sockets over the remaining four, as there were evidently two different discus placed on two layers. Just when the sockets matched one another, there was a loud clanking of metals, and the circular hole on the floor opened.

And there it was. They could see another stairway leading below to the third level of the underground chamber. They descended to this level to reach another large hall. The inlay had uncanny resemblances with chamber inside Egyptian pyramids. There were large stone box-like structures, much like the Egyptian sarcophagus, with intricate inscriptions on stone lids, much like the hieroglyphs. The team, however, could not decipher the script. There were total twelve large boxes, three on each side of the room, placed along a circumference, with a central box with nine sides. The most sacred letter *Aum* was inscribed on the nonagon. There was a head of a snake pointing out from each of the twelve boxes facing towards the central box.

Despite these trying times, the team was in high spirit. Maya was trying to overcome her fear. She studied the numbers carved in the stone and pointed out, 'I have never seen such an arrangement before'. She had a habit of playing with numbers. 'We can place these twelve boxes perfectly in a circle, each with a separation of 30 degrees from the other. The nine sides of the central box can divide this circle in equal proportion of 40 degrees. But when put together, these two arrangements cannot divide a circle.' She further pointed out to the snouts of the snake-heads as they were directed towards the central box. It appeared that the twelve snakes were protecting the central box, and each head was multiplying the strength of the protection. She continued, 'What do we get when we divide the circle with these multiplying powers/ 12 X 9? 360 divided by 12X9 gives 3.333333, recurring till infinity. This is the significance of the sacred number 108. It protects us from all around like the Trinity.'

The team took a moment to absorb the fact. Farah and Virat were curious to discover what was inside those boxes. The insides of the hallway was becoming less breathable every minute. Anjan's torch was shining less brighter. A certain sense of dizziness was setting in. Adi jolted and looked at his team members. He reminded them of the situation they were in. They had to get out of this chamber as early as possible. Suddenly Farah noticed a faint ray of light coming from one corner of the hallway and jumped in excitement. They ran towards the direction of light, and noticed a gentle slope going up. They climbed up the slope carefully. They were astonished to find themselves standing just behind the Shivling within the Sanctum Sanctorum of the temple. Since it was almost past 3:00 pm, it was time for a brief closure of the temple premises as per routine. They were even more surprised to see a familiar face welcoming them in the *mandir prangan*. The priest out-stretched his hands and said, 'My children, You have successfully passed your test. I do not regret showing you the passageway. But remember, you must not disclose what you have witnessed today. I pray to the Almighty for bestowing blessings and success in all your future endeavours.'

The team touched the priest's feet, as he sprinkled some holy water on them and blessed them with *'Vijayee Bhava'*, and they came out of the temple.

The team later came to know that this kind of underground passageway was abundant in Gujarat. If one had to believe the local people, one such underground tunnel system was still present between three important temples. From the Modhera Sun temple, exactly twenty-two miles to the north is Rani ki Vav Temple in Patan, and these two temples are connected by underground tunnels. Those tunnels were as big and wide as to allow passage of two horsemen side by side after leaving space for the infantry. At regular intervals, there were openings for fresh air to be sucked in, and alternative entry and exit points. Again, from Modhera Sun Temple, exactly thirty-five kilometres away to the east was Jasmalnathji Temple, and these temples were also connected by the same kind of underground passage. Thus these three temples formed a perfect right-angled triangle connected underground. Nowadays, people know that the Seiken Tunnel in Japan was considered as the longest underground tunnel, which had a length of about fifty-three kilometres, and was constructed in the late eighties. But, it was incredible to know that such underground tunnels existed in ancient India as well.

Jagannatha

*I*ndradyumna summoned Sage Narada, who was an old friend, and fairly omniscient. He consulted with him regarding the sacrifice of countless horses which was inevitable due to the presence of the dangerous object hidden in the stable. The sage advised him to shrug off his inhibitions because he had undertaken such a humongous task. 'In the meantime', Narada suggested, 'put an idol of Lord Nrusingha in the unfinished temple. People can be distracted from any event of casualty and mayhem, if any, in the name of the most destructive and fiercely Avatar of Lord Vishnu.' He asked the King to make preparations for carving the idols, as he had envisioned in his dreams, from the pyre woods which by then had come near the seashore.

Many carpenters tried to carve out an idol. But their instruments were getting damaged while trying to cut the wood. Then *an old carpenter, weak and frail, offered to accomplish the task. The old man however had two strange conditions. He wanted to work in complete isolation in a closed chamber. The king hesitantly complied to the conditions and handed him the job.*

Queen Gundicha was getting impatient at the delay of the idol carving. Almost, three weeks passed. Although there were sounds of carving in the initial days, it began fading gradually and finally stopped as days passed. She was wary of the old craftsman, and requested the King to get updates on the task. They both approached the closed chamber. There was complete silence. On repeated requests from the King, there was no answer from the carpenter. Anxious to know what really was happening in the chamber, the King broke the door open. To their astonishment, the couple saw half-finished idols of Lord Jagannatha, Lord Balabhadra, and Lady Subhadra. Angry at being interrupted in his task, the carpenter immediately left, never to return. The King was disheartened, he had broken his own promise.

The onlookers were mesmerized to see the Lord in this form, and the king decided to consecrate the idols in their half-finished structures. He also knew that he was running out of time to place the hidden object in a safe and inert place. The king counselled with Lord Brahma for the next procedures. Upon His suggestion, he placed the stone in the hollow of the wooden idol of Lord Jagannatha. He set out a detailed instruction of the entire process for worshipping the Lord. Subsequently, he made a secret society of priests and instructed them for the maintenance of the sacred stone in future. He asked them to replace the wood of the idol after every 8, 12 or 19 years, naming this auspicious ritual as Nabakalebara, depending on the quality of the Daru Brahma, the special Neem wood, to replenish the decaying idol from the effect of the object that was kept inside. This procedure must be carried on a new moon night, with a strong mind to get salvation within one year of performing this act. Also necessary safety protocols should be followed while replacing the Brahma Padartha by being blindfolded and using gloves.

The king had kept his promise to his Lord. He made the most sacred and magnificent temple at Jagannathdham, a perfect place for the Lord to retire and refresh Himself. While doing so, he safeguarded the Brahma Padartha, which could be activated in future to create the ultimate weapon, when time necessitates.

Chapter Seven

SOMNATH SIGHTSEEING

Adi asked Anjan to get their car from the hotel while they waied inside the temple compound for his return.

Just before entering the hotel parking area, Anjan was welcomed by a valet driver who accompanied him to the car. He gently handed over a white envelope to Anjan. There was nothing written on the envelope. Anjan opened the envelope and pulled a paper out. It was blank. Anjan frowned and enquired, 'Who gave you this?' The driver nodded and said that one gentleman told him to deliver the envelope to the team who arrived from Hyderabad. The valet had noticed them during check-in the earlier day. Anjan asked, 'Where is the gentleman?' The driver pointed out his finger to a black car. There was someone sitting inside. As Anjan proceeded towards the car, it revved up, and speeded away.

While Anjan was away, Maya and Farah had already made an itinerary for their afternoon trip. They would first visit the temple in memory of Queen Ahilyabai Holkar, just opposite to the main Somnath temple. This would be followed by the *Triveni Ghat*, a confluence of Hiranya and Kapila rivers, though many believed that the mythical underground river Saraswati also met at the same place. Then they would visit the nearby Shri Ram Mandir, and Prabhas Patan Museum. Finally, after seeing the *Bhalka Teerth*, they would return to their hotel.

By the time Anjan reached, four of them were coming out of the Mata Ahilya temple. Adi took the co-driver's seat as usual. While others were busy boarding and accommodating themselves in the middle and rear seats, Anjan briefed Adi about receiving the white envelope. Adi did not give much importance to the episode. He reacted casually.

The team was resting under the famous Peepal tree at the Bhalka Teerth temple compound. 'This was the place where last of the mortals saw THE Sudarshan Chakra.' Virat started explaining and reminded everyone that it was believed, the Chakra went under the abyss of Mother Earth at the same spot where Lord Krishna died. As Jara, the hunter, was the last person with the Lord, many believed that he carried the Chakra with him. Since after His death, Jara went to Somnath temple and spent his life as a devotee of Lord Shiva, it is believed that he hid the Chakra in the temple. Can this be a reason why every invader who attacked the country invariably paid a visit to Somnath temple in the disguise of looting the temple? Were they trying to find something else?

Adi re-iterated that though it was their first day of sight-seeing, but it was with a purpose. It was a common practice to start a project, which had some links with the past, from Ground Zero. It was necessary for fact-finding and information gathering. And now they were sitting right there. 'Let's start with some facts about the Chakra, and let's see what all we know till date', Adi lead the conversation. 'Since we are on a trip to historical places today from the morning, let's discuss on the philosophical and theological aspects of the Chakra.'

Farah started, 'As per popular belief and as mentioned in the Shree Jagannatha Purana, the Chakra is present along with Lord Jagannatha in Puri. There, the Chakra has been modified into a stump made of neem wood, and is called '*Daru Brahma*'. Though I have never entered the temple, I know that it is placed on the *Ratna Singhasana* on the left-hand side of Lord Jagannatha, along with Lord Balabhadra and Devi Subhadra. There is another story of the presence of the Chakra in Puri, where it has been mentioned that after receiving orders from the Lord to slit the head of Pradyumna, the king of Dwarka who had become extremely malevolent during the end of Dwapar Yuga, the Chakra did not return to the Lord, as it was filled with sorrow and grief, and landed at a place now called *Chakratirtha* in Puri. All these show that the weapon also had parallelly been imagined to possess humane quality with some kind of intelligence built into it. But, I am not sure about the origin of the weapon.'

Maya explained, 'Sajnya, the daughter of Lord Viswakarma, greatest engineer and architect among the Gods, was married to the Sun God Surya. One day, she complained to her father that she could no more bear the extreme heat and radiance of her husband. In order to help her daughter, Lord Viswakarma curtailed Surya's power by one-eighth. The remaining stardust was used to make three powerful objects – the *Trishul* for Lord Shiva, the *Chakra* for Lord Vishnu and the *Pushpak Vimana* for Kuber, which was later taken away forcefully by his half-brother Ravana. Another source regarding the origin of Chakra mentions a beautiful saga. Once, Vishnu meditated for a very long time at the Manikarnika Ghat in Kashi in order to please Lord Shiva. He arranged one thousand lotuses, and offered one lotus every day. After nine hundred and ninety-nine days, on the last day, He could not find any lotus. Seeing this, He attempted to offer one of his eyes to Shiva, as His eyes were as beautiful as lotuses. Lord Shiva was pleased by His penance, and appeared before Him. He asked Him for any boon which He would grant. Lord Vishnu desired for a powerful celestial weapon with which He could kill all the demons and bring back the equilibrium in the universe. Shiva then gifted Him the Sudarshan Chakra. It had the power to impede any attack from the opponent, and would return to the Lord only after accomplishing its task. Interestingly, Lord Vishnu had to do a second meditation in order to acquire the strength to hold it. This shows that it was such a powerful weapon. It had the Power of the Sun itself, and yet, is also considered a weapon with consciousness.'

Anjan joined in, 'I have heard that the Chakra had two discs that revolved at two opposite directions. Each of the discs had one hundred and eight serrated edges. It revolved in high speed and could spew fire on a flight. It was always held on the right index finger of Lord Vishnu and Lord Krishna. This disc used to spin on its own without touching or resting on the finger. It was called Sudarshan, as it looked beautiful when not used, but it was a deadly weapon that could create havoc and disaster.'

'In Rigveda,' Adi added, 'the Chakra has been mentioned as a symbol of Vishnu, just like the *Lingam* of Lord Shiva. Later, the Chakra was imagined as an *Ayudhpurush*, an anthropomorphic form of the weapon. In this form, it was called *Chakraperumal* or *Chakrathazhwar*, a fierce form of Lord Vishnu, and was worshipped as a separate deity. Thus we get an alternate picture of having an independent entity of the weapon with its own intelligence and existence.'

Virat said, with a face full of emotion and anguish, 'There is always science in the Vedas, which we are not able to decipher till date, and term them as myths and fantasies. These scriptures were composed of speeches from the Gods. They were so hard to comprehend by mankind that it was necessary to compose the Puranas, taking the ideas of the Vedas, so that the common people could understand them easily. And these necessitated the Puranas to incorporate some extra facts which later became mythologies. Lord Krishna was a historical figure, which many people believe as a myth. Thanks to Western knowledge which have till now not been able to prove His existence, just like King Ashoka. Ashoka was also considered a mythical figure, a mythological King, before the discovery of Ashoka *Stambha*, and many other inscriptions all around the subcontinent.' His eyes filled with hatred and frustration as he continued, 'The West has the practice to term any native history before the birth of Christ as mere mythology. Situations worsened upon the incessant attacks of central Asian invaders.' He remembered how his father had told him stories of invasions. 'One

Mughal ruler had once thrown some historians from the Red Fort in front of hungry tigers, as they did not agree to write history as dictated by him, History has always been *His story'*. He continued, 'How come such accurate geographical locations associated with the life incidents of Krishna are still available in so many different places? Mathura - the birthplace of Krishna, Vrindavan – where He spent his childhood days, Nidhiban – where He used to play along with His friends, Dwarka – where He built his own kingdom, this place where we are sitting right now which is considered to be His final resting place - are still existing till present day. Also, it is quite impossible for the writer, the great seer Guru Vedavyasa, to imagine and compose all these details with so much accuracy had he not visualized all those incidents happening before his own eyes.'

The discussion continued quite long. The sun had already set. It was dark in this western part of the country. The team retired to their hotel rooms. At the dinner table, they finalized their plan for the next day. They would check out from the hotel early morning, and would travel to Dwarka in their car. There, they might retrieve some information, decode hidden clues related to their mission.

Earlier, during check-in, they had not disclosed their true identities at the reception of the hotel. They all registered their names as casual visitors, and showed their general Photo Identity Cards, and not their professional identities. But there was something unusual about the hotel. Every time they would order anything, one specific room service boy would come and wait for them. Now, at the dinner table, the same man was serving them food. It was he who came to their rooms to serve breakfast in the morning. He was over friendly, and tried to linger with them unnecessarily. Adi, on remembering the envelope incident, described by Anjan at afternoon, truncated their discussion at dinner table. Everybody completed their food, and bid good night to proceed to their respective rooms. They would be having a long journey in the next morning.

Replacement

Now that the first eighteen years passed, the black deity was turning into white, while the other two deities were turning black. This was a clear indication that the time had come to replace the woods of the deities, and craft new deities in their place, a practise which was propheszied by King Indradyumna himself. It was time for Nabakalebara.

It was an intercalary month, an Adhikmasa, when two lunar months of Asadha fell in the same year as per the calendar. This was a rare occasion that might happen once every twelve years, but this time, the interval was occurring in the nineteenth year.

A group of one hundred servitors, who were called daitas, headed by their Dalapati, arrived at the King's palace and described the change in appearance of the idols. The King consulted with Rajaguru. As per advise of the Rajaguru, the king offered each of them *a betel nut and asked them to find new trees from which new idols would be built. The group took blessings from both the King and the Rajaguru and headed for Banajaga Yatra in pursuit of wood.*

The team was walking barefoot in the scorching sun. After travelling about fifty kilometres, they reached Deuli Matha and decided to take rest for the night. On the next morning, they reached Kakatpur Mangala Temple. Four senior members in the group suggested that they should seek blessings and ask the Devi to guide them in right direction in which they should further proceed, in order to find the perfect woods.

The history of Mangala Devi is quite famous. It was the main deity in the temple of the infamous Sri Lankan King Ravana. He was a great devotee of Mangala Mata and became supreme powerful by her blessings. After his defeat in the hands of Lord Rama, a Sadhaba who was accompanying the Lord on His return journey, brought the Goddess to Utkala from Sri Lanka. But he was unable to find a rightful place to sanctify her and immersed her in the nearby Prachi river.

Once a sailor was crossing the river on a stormy day. It was heavily raining and he could not control his dinghy in the cloudburst. Rain was accompanied by strong gusts of wind and the sailor lost control of the vessel despite his skilful manoeuvres throughout the whole day. Night arrived, but he was still stuck in the middle of the river. He was completely exhausted. Unable to move forward, he tried taking a nap. While he was dozing in the early hours of the dawn, the Goddess arrived in his dream and asked him to take her out of the water. He woke up immediately and dived in the river at the exact location as instructed by Her, and found the deity. The deity was established in a temple in the neighbouring Mangalpur village. After the rituals were over, he was begun to sail his boat. Suddenly, he noticed a black crow diving at the same location in the river from where the idol was dug out. He waited patiently for the crow to come to the surface. Hours turned into days, and days became weeks. But the crow never came out of the water. The boatman understood that it was all part of the divine game of the Goddess, and christened the spot as Kaka-Ataka. The Goddess then came to be known as Kakatpur Mangala by the locals.

The assembly of servitors waited for the whole day as the idol of Mangala Devi was not present in sanctum. They believed their deity was taking a tour of the universe. There was a stone bed in front of the Vimana. The bed was beautifully made so as to welcome the Goddess after the completion of a long, tiresome journey. When night arrived, they however could not keep themselves awake, and dozed off in deep slumber. At early dawn, during Brahmamuhurta, the Goddess appeared in their dreams and directed them to the place where they would find the required woods to build new idols. When they opened their eyes, they were surprised to see the bed being undone and worn out, as if someone had retired there.

They continued their journey and arrived at a village where they found a neem tree, which was reddish in colour. There was a circular depression in the centre of the trunk and a symbol of chakra embedded on the opposite side. They apprehended that this was the tree for the Sudarshan to be rebuilt.

They went in the second direction at a distance and found a neem tree with a yellowish hue. It had five clear branches which expanded like petals of lotus. This was the tree for Subhadra.

In another direction, they found a third neem tree with its trunk light brown in colour. It had seven branches which formed a canopy in the shape of a seven-headed serpent. This was the tree for Balabhadra.

Finally, they arrived at a place where they found a tree as was prescribed in scriptures. That neem tree had a dark red coloured trunk and it stood perfectly straight in the air, about twelve cubits high, with four clear outstretched branches. It was standing right in the middle of the intersection of three roads, just beside a reservoir filled with clear water. They were sure that the tree was meant for Lord Jagannatha.

They covered all the trees with pure white clothes and fell them religiously, and carried them back amidst the beating of drums and kartals. They brought the logs in Koili Baikuntha, where these would be kept temporarily till the carving of new idols were completed.

Chapter Eight

TRAVEL TO DWARKA

The distance from Somnath to Dwarka by road was two hundred and thirty-three kilometres. It would take nearly four hours to reach there by road with a standard driving experience. The team boarded their car. They had completed their breakfast early and checked out of the hotel. They planned to reach Dwarka well before the evening.

The vehicle was a perfect choice for long trips. It was the latest model of Range Rover SE, with a 33.27 cm touchscreen infotainment system, through which navigating to the destination was easy for any person on the wheels. There was a wireless charging facility with phone signal boosters. Also, it had three-zone climate control for the comfort of passengers seated in all rows. The car was equipped with a four-wheel driving feature.

The road from Somnath to Dwarka was spectacular. It was the National Highway 51, commonly known as the Coastal Way. It ran parallel to the coastline of Arabian Sea, all along, throughout the entire journey.

In about an hour, they reached Madhavpur beach. It was a beautiful beach with white sand and blue waters. They decided to have a tea break there. Many tourists were enjoying with their families and friends on the beach. Some children were enjoying camel and horse rides. This was one of the cleanest beaches in India. The experience of enjoying the sunset from this beach would be a memory to cherish.

At a short distance from the beach, they reached a place where mythology and history put forth an impeccable bouquet of rich incidents from the past. The place was called Madhuvan. This was the place where the infamous Madhu demon was killed by Lord Vishnu with His mace, a rare incident where the Lord used His all-powerful *Koumadaki* mace in a close combat with the demon. Also, this was the place where Lord Krishna and Rukmini got married. The princess had sent a secret message to Him, after she was threatened to be abducted by Sishupala and his ally Jarasandha. People speculate this as the first written love letter in the world. Rukmini was desperate to flee as she did not like Sishupala from any aspect. Sishupala was notorious for his tyranny towards the residents of his kingdom. Rukmini's father had already arranged their marriage. She asked Krishna to come to Amaravati, her father's kingdom, to rescue her. Rukmini eloped with

Krishna from Amaravati and reached Madhuvan. Krishna and Rukmini spent a night there. The Sun and the Moon God witnessed their marriage, the next day. This place, along with the temples of Rukmini, Krishna, the Sun and the Moon, were now protected by the Archaeological Survey of India.

On the way, they crossed a small bridge where the beautiful Madhuvanti river was meeting the Arabian Sea.

Within an hour from Madhavpur beach, they reached Porbandar. This was a place of fame around the world as it was the birthplace of Mahatma Gandhi. Both Gandhiji and his wife Kasturba's ancestral houses were at Porbandar. The Government had built a *Kirti Mandir* in commemoration of Gandhiji. As he believed in peaceful co-existence and brotherhood among people belonging to various faiths, the Mandir was built likewise to accommodate the architectural styles of Muslims, Buddhists, Christians, Sikhs and Hindus.

Porbandar and its adjoining areas were also dotted with many other places of interest. The famous Jambuvan caves were just fifteen kilometres away. It was believed that Jambuvan and Lord Krishna had fought non-stop for twenty-seven days owing to the dispute over possession of *Syamantaka Mani*. The mani was claimed to have magical properties. It turned any object into gold upon touching. Being blessed with immortality, Jambuvan was fighting relentlessly. He was also granted invincibility in Treta Yuga by Lord Rama. Though he fought valiantly, he was defeated. Jambuvan realized the true identity of his opponent, Lord Krishna. He was filled with remorse. Krishna forgave him. In gratitude, he offered a marriage proposal for his daughter Jamvanti with the Lord, and Krishna married her within the cave.

There was Sandipani Mandir near Porbandar Airport, in memory of Sage Sandipan of Ujjain, who was a teacher of Lord Krishna and his best friend Sudama. At present, there is a beautiful Radha Krishna temple built within the complex. An orphanage and a school for the downtrodden had also been established in the vicinity.

The famous Sudama Ji Temple was at the heart of Porbandar. In earlier times, Porbandar was known as Sudamapuri. This was the place where Lord Krishna's dearest friend used to live. A temple had been built at his ancestral house, where the idols of Sudama Ji, his wife Susheela Devi, Lord Krishna and Devi Radha were placed side by side on the same altar.

There was so much more to explore. However as the team was on an official trip, and had a limited timeframe, they could not afford to have a stoppage there.

After leaving Porbandar, they took two hours to reach Dwarka. Adi initiated a small discussion during the journey. He described a video which he had recently watched on YouTube. He said, 'What I saw was a Ring Chakra. It is a circular metal disc, much like a circular sickle, with a sharp outer edge along the circumference and a blunt inner edge in the middle. It can be held by hand, and thrown at the approaching enemy. It was a particular throwing weapon used by the Sikhs against the Europeans. It was deadly for the clueless Europeans as it was a rotating weapon which created havoc and confusion in the enemy line. It varied in sizes from two inches to six inches in diameter.'

'Yes, I also know this weapon used by the Sikhs.' Farah affirmed as she googled some images while she spoke. When she was done with her search, she brought up her mobile phone to show a picture to everyone, and exclaimed, 'Also, Akshay Kumar wore such weapons on his turban in the "*Kesariya*" movie, see this.' Everyone looked at the picture on her phone which was a turban, stuffed in the upper end to make it stand like a tall hat with a pointy end. There were five circular hand-held weapons as described by Adi earlier. It amused them all.

Fig.5 : *Mid-19th century Nihang turban from Lahore. Cotton over a wicker frame and steel overlaid with gold. "A tall conical turban provided convenient transportation for a number of sharp steel quoits — edged weapons hurled to lethal effect by the practised hand of the Akalis." (source: Wikipedia, Chalram, https://en.m.wikipedia.org/wiki/Chakram)*

Farah continued as if she was visualizing some memories from her past, 'Such kinds of *Chakras* are commonly used in a format of Sri Lankan martial art, called *Angampora*. People believe that this gave birth to *Kalaripayattu*, a special form of martial art that can be traced back to ancient India. However, the Sri Lankan format is special with its own characteristics. The local people believe that *Angampora* was also practised during the times of Ravana. So, the first-ever use of Chakra was done by the Asuras and the *Yakkhas*.'

Adi nodded in affirmation as he continued, 'The Europeans noted that the Sikhs wore long conical turbans and mounted these circular weapons on them. Even in Akbar Nama, a sixteenth-century text, written by Abul Faz'l ibn Mubarak, the court historian and biographer of Mughal emperor Akbar the Great, we see pictures of such weapons being used in war. It was twirled on the index finger and hurled at great speed on the opponent. People generally believe that such a weapon was used by the Sikhs only, and came into practice around 1500 AD. But in 2014, a stone pillar was discovered underneath a temple in South India. It was dated around 1200 to 1300 AD, and there were inscriptions of such ring chakras on it. So, this weapon must be of use in much older times also.'

Virat added, 'References of Sudarshan Chakra can be seen outside of India also. The concept of Sudarshan Chakra spread to the west, as well as to the east. Many artifacts depicting the Chakra have been discovered in Afghanistan, that stretched as far as Bactria. A fourth-century seal has been discovered in Bactria where a king was shown worshipping Lord Vishnu. There was a huge Sudarshan Chakra almost half the size of the king engraved on the seal. A number of antiquities have been discovered in Thailand which look like present-day rotors having a great aerodynamic design, with cutting blades. These are called Chakram or Chakri in their local language. Even the present ruling dynasty of Thailand is called the Chakri dynasty. The royal insignia of Thailand is a fusion of the Chakra of Vishnu and the Trishul of Shiva. Thailand was earlier known as Ayutthaya, derived from Ayodhya, and the kings were called Rama. People of Thailand still believe that the original Chakra is held by the royals in their palace, and they are considered to be the descendants of God.' He googled some keywords and showed them a picture on his phone.

Fig. 6 : 5000 years old model of the Sudarshana Chakra discovered in Shahr-e-Sukhteh in the Iran-Afghanistan border (source: Wikipedia, Shahr-e Sukhteh, https://en.wikipedia.org/wiki/Shahr-e_Sukhteh)

'This demonstrates the impact of our *Sanatana Dharma* over large geographies of Asia, and also over major parts of other continents. Gods and goddesses influenced by the *Sanatana Dharma* were worshipped in many areas of the world in the ancient period. They were powerful with various kinds of weapons which we are trying to rediscover at present.' Maya inferred as she was enjoying the scenic beauty along the road.

On the way, they could see huge wind mills to harness electricity, which was as picturesque as ever. These were under the Government of India's Green Energy Mission, currently operated by Tata Powers.

They saw a beautiful peacock crossing the road, and halted to take some snaps. All of them cherished the road-side scenic beauty. They thoroughly enjoyed the blue waves of the Arabian Sea on the left, and lush-green landscape on the right. The scenic journey ended as they reached their hotel at Dwarka.

Nabakalebara

As the news of the arrival of Nyasa Daru, the newly chopped logs retrieved by the team, reached Indradyumna, he came with Rajaguru to verify the logs. Rajaguru was appointed to follow rituals as per customs. The revered woods were worshipped daily, prasad was offered. This continued until the immediate full moon day. On the auspicious Purnima, which they termed as Debasnan Purnima, the new logs were bathed. The original idols in the main temples were also given a bath on that Snan Purnima day, and the temple was closed for forty-five days. They called it a ritual of Maha Anasara.

During the first fifteen days of that Krishnapaksha, various discussions and preparations were made regarding the carving of the new idols. Then, at the beginning of the Shukla Paksha, the Maharanas, who were master carpenters commenced their toughest task *of recreating the Lord within a timeframe of twenty-one days. Working day and night, focused with complete devotion to the Lord, they built new idols which were perfect replicas of the old ones. They circum-ambulated the new idols and brought them in a secret chamber within the main temple, where the old idols were already carried out from the sanctum sanctorum and placed before them. The new and the old idols were kept face-to-face with each other. It was midnight of the new moon day. The main priest got himself blindfolded, wrapped his hands with thick layers of special clothes, and started the initiation of transfer of the Brahmapadartha from the heart of the old idol of Jagannatha to the new idol. It was pitch dark in the entire place. The priest was unable to fathom the shape of the object that he had just transferred, but it was too heavy, while it almost felt as smooth and soft as a bunny, and it was rapidly pulsating with life.*

The next morning, the old idols were declared dead. They were carried on chariots to Koili Baikuntha for burial. That followed the observation of Asouch for ten days when no one was allowed to approach the Patali. On the eleventh day, the servites who were associated with the funeral obsequies took a holy bath. On the twelfth day, a ceremonial feast was held and Mahaprasad was distributed among the devotees.

Following the completion of the funeral formalities, the new idols, which were still kept inside the temple were covered in a protective covering of Saptavarana. Only a selected few were allowed to go near them. Saptavarana comprised of sandal paste, camphor, musk and Kumkum wrapped in a red silk cloth, and a white silk cloth soaked in sesame oil. Painting of the idols were then done according to the skin colours of the Gods and Goddesses. The whole procedure lasted for another fortnight.

After that, the main priest performed the Netrotsava, or the opening of the eyes of the Lords by drawing the eye-lids. This was the final touch in the whole life-infusing ritual for the new idols. The following day, the main doors of the temple were opened to the public for Naba Jauban Darshan.

This was the start of the celebration. The next day, three magnificent chariots, beautifully decorated, would carry the idols for a ceremonial visit to the house of Queen Gundicha, whom, by now, people had started venerating as the Mausi of Lord Jagannatha. People took part in the grand procession and celebrated and chanted the names of the Lord. The Lord would reside in that garden temple for the next eight days.

Thus the tradition of Rathayatra started and continued for generations.

Chapter Nine

DWARKA SIGHTSEEING

The team reached their hotel at Dwarka shortly before sunset. It was a wonderful journey. They planned to spend some time together while having their evening tea, before retiring for the day.

They started discussing about the place. Virat took a sip from his cup, and exclaimed, 'Archaeologists have discovered a nine-thousand-year old city. Guess what, it is not the Atlantis, but Dwarka, the resident city of Krishna.'

Farah reminded all about the meaning of Dwarka. She elaborated, 'Krishna reached Dwarka with his eighteen friends from Mathura. The city was fortified with high walls on each side, to defend its people from any attack. The city was accessible only by some strategic gates and doors or '*Dwar*', for which the city was named Dwarka – the city with doors. As per scientific specimens gathered right from the creation till the flooding of Dwarka, one can say that this is not a mythology, but an untold history which has become obscured in our minds. India is the cradle of one of the most ancient civilizations in the world. Dwarka was a historical city in India, not a fictional place as many people believe.'

Anjan, who was all along busy on the wheels, got a chance to take part in the discussion at last. He interrupted, 'But, what can be the cause of this submergence?'

'Dwarka was founded by Krishna after He left Mathura. It was built at the confluence of Gomti river and the Arabian Sea,' Maya replied, 'it was a huge and planned city, much better than most of the modern-day cities. It was one of the most developed places in the Indian subcontinent at contemporary times. After Krishna killed His maternal uncle, the cruel king of Mathura, Kansa's father-in-law Jarasandha kept attacking Mathura repeatedly. Though the battles were all won by Him, on the eighteenth time while the battle was ongoing, He realized that this will never stop Jarasandha from attacking Mathura again in future. So, Krishna fled from the battle-field earning the name *Ranchor*. Krishna then relocated and settled in Dwarka for the safety and well-being of His subjects. Prolonged war had brought unrest and distress among them. They faced a problem upon reaching Dwarka. How would they build a fort using soft sand by the sea-side? Krishna realized that hard rocky surface was required, as present under that specific sea-bed. It is said that Krishna reclaimed some portions of land from the sea, after pleading the Sea God. The city was built within a single night by Viswakarma, the God of Architecture and Engineering. This walled city was a masterpiece of architecture and art by itself, with its beautiful white mansions covered with gold on the high domes, roads adorned with beautiful flowering plants on its sides, fountains at the crossroads filled with aroma due to lotuses blossoming in the water. But it submerged in the sea within a week of the death of Krishna. As per some researchers, it was bombarded and destroyed by Salwa, with his huge army. He himself attacked Dwarka from his powerful Vimana while flying in the air, which he received from Lord Shiva. But, the most accepted views behind the subsidence of Dwarka in the sea, as per the context of Mahabharata, were two main reasons. One was the curse given by Gandhari to Krishna, for the death of all of her sons in the war of Kurukshetra. She cursed that everything which He possessed, including each member of His clan, will be destroyed. Another reason was due to the curse given by the sages to Samba, the son of Krishna, when Samba ridiculed them in the disguise of a woman. The city submerged almost after thirty-six years since the end of Mahabharata war. The remains of the city are still available in the depths of the Arabian Sea. After extensive excavations done in the region, artifacts as old as nine thousand years have been recovered.' Maya elaborated, as she visualized the whole episodes from past.

Adi put some scientific facts in support of Farah and Maya. He said, 'People believed that the oldest city on earth was the Atlantis. But in 1970, some Indian Air Force pilots noticed something under the waters of the Arabian Sea at the place between Dwarka and Bet Dwarka. By 1979, the ASI took an initiative to explore the site. Though some antiquities were recovered, extensive research could not be done due to lack of funds. In 2005, the then Director of ASI took an initiative for a detailed exploration in order to re-discovering the Dwarka, and collected relics from both off-shore and on-shore. This time, he collected some coins and potteries, which when carbon-dated appeared to be about nine thousand years old. Some portions of the old wall of Dwarka, about three hundred and sixty metres long, was also discovered under the waters. A triangular anchor and remains of ship wreckage were discovered too, which proved that it was a major port of the region. Also, some Roman coins were recovered, which showed it had trade relations with the Western world. The main reason for the flooding is believed to be the rising of the sea level. The place was already a low-lying area, being reclaimed from the sea. Others cite climate change due to pollution as a result of heavy urbanization. Also, overgrazing of farmlands caused havoc for the place. Another popular theory is that Krishna, being the God Himself, and the most intelligent and knowledgeable among all in His time, already knew of an earthquake and resultant tsunami in this place. He tried to rebuild the world anew. It was an obvious way to put an end for his own people, who did not take part in the Great War, and became vicious'.

The team started their next day early. They planned to visit both Dwarka and Beyt Dwarka on the same day. Generally, visitors cover this itinerary in two days. But time was limited for them as they were on a mission.

At first, they went to the Rukmini temple which was nearly two kilometres from their hotel. Many other visitors had already arrived there. They parked their car in the parking area, which was quite large.

Anjan enquired, 'Tell me something about Rukmini and the significance of this place.'

It was Farah who first answered. She had a deep knowledge on historical stories. She said, 'Rukmini was first and queen consort of Lord Krishna. She is also considered as an incarnation of Goddess Lakshmi. We already know the story about the marriage of Rukmini and Lord Krishna. After her marriage with Krishna, Rukmini felt very proud of herself thinking that she was the most beautiful girl in the world, as the Lord Himself came to her rescue after receiving a single letter. Krishna noticed her ego, but did not let her understand. He had some other plans.'

'See, this is His greatness. The whole mankind was equal to Him. He did not provide any extra advantage to even His most near and dear ones, and always treated everyone equally,' Maya interrupted.

Farah continued, 'To remove her ego, Krishna invited Rishi Durvasa to the grand feast organized for their marriage ceremony. The Rishi accepted the invitation, while putting forth a condition that he will not arrive by a chariot that is drawn by any animal. Krishna, seeing no other option to please His Guru, asked His wife Rukmini to accompany him, and the two started to draw the chariot by their own hands. But Rukmini, being a princess, brought up in royal abundance and opulence, did not have strength for such an arduous task. On the way, she felt very exhausted and thirsty and sought help from her husband. Krishna dug a hole in the earth with His toe to bring out some water, to quench her thirst. Rukmini drank some water. But the Rishi, riding on the chariot got furious seeing this. He shouted angrily, how could she drink water without offering him first! He cursed that henceforth there would be no potable water available in this area. Also there would be no water available for farming. Moreover, the Rishi cursed the couple that they would not be able to consummate their marriage for the next twelve years. Rukmini was shattered. This is the place where she spent twelve years in meditation and prayer after that incident.'

Farah and Maya entered the temple to pray and pay respect to Rukmini Devi, while the other three were busy planning for their next destination, Beyt Dwarka.

From there, the team reached Okha. This was the last village en route the island. One would reach Karachi, Pakistan when travelled straight from there. The team booked a boat to reach Beyt Dwarka. It was almost thirteen kilometres away from the mainland. The island was visible in the distance, and it took about twenty minutes to reach there. They could see a bridge that was getting constructed, which would be open to the public in another two or three years, and it would be possible to reach there by a car from Okha. After getting down from the boat, they had to walk for five minutes to reach the Dwarkadheesh temple. The temple was beautiful and large, and they paid a visit to Lord Krishna, worshipped there as Dwakadheesh. Mobile and video photography were prohibited inside the temple, and they had to deposit their belongings in the cloak room before entering the temple.

Maya informed all, 'This is where Lord Krishna met his childhood friend Sudama. Sudama gave Him rice to eat, hence, rice is still offered as a *prasad* to Lord Krishna in this temple.'

Their next destination was a temple called Hanuman Daandi. The temple was dedicated to Lord Hanuman. There were idols of Lord Hanuman and his son Makardhwaj inside the temple. They were quite surprised, as they all knew that Lord Hanuman was a life-long celibate.

Adi asked the main priest to clarify their doubts.

The Purohit depicted the story in details. He said, 'Hanuman Ji went to the sea to drench his tail after Lanka was set ablaze. Exasperated from the heat of the fire, He was sweating profusely. Some drops of His sweat fell into the mouth of a *Makar.* Hanuman Ji was completely unaware of this. Later, that crocodile gave birth to Makardhwaj. He was raised by Ahiravana, the brother of Ravana. If you look carefully, you will see a speciality in the idol of Makardhwaj in this temple. When Sri Rama and His brother Lakshmana went to Lanka in search of Sita, kidnapped by Ravana, they were captured by AhiRavana. He was the king of *Pataal-Loka*, the land of the netherworlds. This temple is located at the entry of the Pataal-Loka.'

Anjan was surprised by all these facts and exclaimed, 'This place is far away from Sri Lanka. How could AhiRavana capture them here? And where is this Pataal-Loka? What is its connection with these demons?'

The priest continued, 'After the abduction of Rama and Lakshmana, Hanuman Ji started searching for them. He scoured every corner of the known world, and came to this place. Makardhwaj was standing guard at the entrance of Pataal-Loka. The duo did not have any idea about each other. Makardhwaj resisted and challenged Hanuman Ji who was trying to trespass. As Hanuman Ji was adamant in entering the Loka, a duel ensued between them, which continued for several days. There was no clear winner. Baffled at the outcome, Hanuman Ji asked the guard to reveal his identity. The guard introduced himself as the son of Hanuman. Hanuman Ji was taken aback, He did not believe his words. He meditated for a brief period and could visualize the whole incident with his *Gyan Chakshu.* He acknowledged Makardhwaj and accepted him. Makardhwaj subsequently helped his father and showed the entry to the Pataal-Loka. Hanuman Ji killed the mighty demon King,

AhiRavana in Pataal-Loka and rescued Rama and Lakshmana from his captivity. The duel between father and son however did not happen with their usual maces, but with sticks or *Daandi*. That is why this temple is called Hanuman Daandi.'

Virat asked, 'But why Makardhwaj is looking quite taller than his father?'

The priest replied, 'Hanuman Ji's idol is decreasing in height by the width of a grain every year as if, He is descending to Pataal-Loka, while the height of Makardhwaj's idol is increasing at the same rate as if, he is emerging from Pataal-Loka. This is the reason for the difference in their heights. This is a unique representation of Hanuman Ji and the only temple of Makardhwaj.'

They thanked the priest for this elaborate story and returned to Okha.

They travelled another nineteen kilometres from Okha to reach Gopi Talav. There they met with the chief priest who explained the significance of Gopi Talav.

The priest started narrating with his closed eyes, and hands folded in reverence, 'Once, sixteen thousand Gopis from Mathura came to meet their childhood friend Krishna, residing then at Dwarka. During their return to Mathura, Krishna appointed Arjuna, His cousin and a great warrior, to ensure their safety. Arjuna accompanied the Gopis. On their way back, they stopped at this Talav for a bath. While Arjuna was resting under a tree, he was attacked by the local forest tribes, called the Bhils. They tied Arjuna to the tree and snatched away all his weapons. Seeing Arjuna in such a helpless condition, the Gopis realised that there was no one to protect them. They decided to sacrifice their lives rather than getting enslaved by the ruthless henchmen. They sacrificed their lives in the Talav. The Gopis were so beautiful and beloved by Lord Krishna that the clay of the pond became sandalwood after this. It is this clay which is used on the forehead of Krishna in the name of Gopichandan.'

Then they went to Mulvel or Momai Beach which was eleven kilometres from Gopi Talav. The road was empty with beautiful greenery on both sides. The sea was visible in a short distance, and the descending road seemed to vanish straight into the sea. Anjan parked the car nearby, and they started walking on the sea beach. They could see the temple of Momai Mata on the beach. Farah felt rejuvenated and said, 'See, the beach is quite different from other sea beaches. It is not sandy, and there are so many sea shells lying here.' She started collecting some sea-shells, while the others started strolling on the beautiful crescent-shaped sea beach. The waves were not high, and the clear water was washing their feet. Adi said, 'I think that the sea bed will be steep if we go further.' Maya admiringly looked at Adi and said, 'I wish to sit on one of these rocks and see this exquisite view uninterrupted – such is the tranquillity and serenity of this place.' The horizon seemed unworldly. They were cherishing every moment. The beach was desolated, yet aesthetically pleasing. It was completely devoid of the din and bustle of city lives. Anjan and Virat were talking among themselves. Farah approached them with her hand full of sea-shells. Virat, while taking a beautiful miniature conch from her hand, said to Anjan, 'We could have experienced the magnificent sunrise from here.' Anjan pointed to the forest nearby, and said, 'There might be many peacocks in this forest. They would be roaming on this beach every evening.' It was exhilarating break for all of them. They felt quite rejuvenated despite a long, hectic exploration.

Next, they went to Nageshwar Jyotirlinga temple which was about ten kilometres from the beach. Maya started describing the background about the temple on the course of journey. 'This is eighth in the list of twelve Jyotirlingas. In ancient times, this whole place was a dense forest, and a demon named Daaruk used to live here. Supriya, a great devotee of Lord Shiva, came into this forest to meditate. But the demon continuously threatened and tormented her. He would throw flesh and blood in *yajna kunda* and make it impure. Supriya often, could not complete her rituals. However, she tolerated all these tortures and was deeply focused in her meditation. Lord Shiva and Parvati Mata were moved by her devotion and appeared before her in the form of a pair of snakes and killed the demon. This was uncommon, as one does not generally have the fortune of seeing Lord Shiva and Parvati Mata together.'

They prayed to Lord Shiva and assembled outside the temple. Adi looked at his watch and said, 'It is 4:30 now. We have to skip the Shivrajpur beach, which is another fifteen kilometres from here. Let us visit the great Dwarkadheesh temple directly. It is almost sixteen kilometres from here, and will take about half an hour to reach.'

They were now standing on the banks of the Gomti river. The great Dwarkadheesh temple was visible at a distance from there. The confluence of the Gomti river with the Arabian Sea was just about three hundred metres away. The confluence presented a magnificent view as the gentle white waters of Gomti intermingled with blue rough waters of the sea. The temple remained closed from one o'clock in the afternoon till five in the evening, as that was the resting time of the Lord. So, they had to wait for some time before the gates of the temple were reopened for visitors. Inside the temple, the main deity of Lord Krishna was dressed as a King. Once they entered the temple, all doubts, questions, confusions from their minds seemed to fade away, creating a tranquil state of mind. They were vibing with the soothing atmosphere of the place.

Anjan asked, 'Hey, please tell me the significance of this place as well.'

'You have experienced it yourself,' Maya was quick to reply as she rolled her eyes. 'One always returns from this temple calm and composed. We are feeling quite relaxed and happy after visiting Lord Krishna.'

Farah added, 'As far as I know, this temple is believed to be built by the fourth generation of the Lord. Pradyumna was the son of Sri Krishna. Pradyumna's son was Aniruddha, whose son Vajranabha built this temple in memory of his great-grandfather. It is one of the *"Char-Dhams"*. Also, it is one of the *"Sapta-Pur"* temples. After Krishna left Gokul, Vrindavan, Braj and Mathura, this was the only place left with his legacy. His elder brother Balarama had received this piece of land as a wedding gift when he married Revati, the daughter of King Revat. Revati was from a different timeline, and during that time her father was the king of the entire earth. The fifty-two metres high flag atop the main dome of the temple is hoisted five times every day. The temple is built in a fashion to house all the family members of Lord Krishna. This includes the house of Mata Devaki, and the *"Rani-vas"*, which is the house of Krishna's wives. Balaram resides on the left side of Krishna's temple, while His son and grandson reside on the right.'

Virat reminded all about the incidents that happened in Dwarka related to Lord Krishna and Rukmini as a couple. 'As per the curse of Rishi Durvasa, no farming can be done in the areas lying within twenty kilometres radius around the temple, till date.'

'Yes, that is the reason why all forty-two villages adjoining this area are barren till present day,' Maya replied. 'Nowadays, it has become a practice to keep arrangements for rain-water harvesting for anyone who builds a house here in this locality.'

'We have visited Dwarkadheesh temple earlier at Beyt Dwarka. Lord Krishna is called Dwarkadheesh here too. Why is that? What is the difference between the two?', Anjan enquired.

Maya had answer to all his queries. She replied in an affirming voice, 'The temple where we are standing now is the royal court of Lord Krishna. The one we visited at Beyt Dwarka was His residence, more likely His queen's residence. There is one more difference. The idol here is believed to have emerged naturally. But at Beyt Dwarka, Mata Rukmini sculpted the idol with her own hands. However, there is one similarity between the two. Both the temples are open for visitors from seven and a half in the morning till half an hour past the noon, and again from five till eight in the evening.'

Adi exclaimed, 'Have you seen the deity of Lord Krishna closely? His eyes are almost closed. This is uncommon. Why is it so?'

Virat was ready with the answer. He replied, 'During the Mughal period, people were very apprehensive of repeated invasions similar to attacks on other temples. So, the head priest took the idol and hid it inside a well for safe-keeping. After some time when the fear of attack subsided, one night the Lord appeared in the dream of the priest and asked to bring Him out on a certain prescribed date and time. But, the priest, excited upon getting a direct command of the Lord, could not wait further. He brought out the idol from the well before the prescribed date. When he looked at the idol he was taken aback. He could hear the voice of the Lord whispering in his ears. The Lord said, "My eyes are closed as you have brought me out while I was still asleep." The priest was aggrieved by his mistake and could not think of an alternate option. He decided to consecrate the idol inside the temple in closed eye condition. This is the reason why we see the idol's eyes, closed. But actually, there is a hair-line opening in between the eye lids through which the Lord can see all His devotees.'

They hailed the Lord together, 'Jai Sri Krishna, Jai Sri Dwarkadheesh.'

While they were roaming about the temple premises, Maya and Farah described the famous *Mangal Aarti* which was held every morning at six and a half for five minutes. They also discussed about the traditional ritual of *"Tula-Daan"* in the morning. The story behind the ritual was very interesting. 'Lord Krishna, once, weighed himself in gold and donated that gold to Maharshi Narada,' Maya said. 'Nowadays, devotees weigh themselves or their family members in seven types of *anaaj* to perform the *Tula-Daan*,' Farah added.

The team then approached towards the beach. Badhkeswar Mahadev temple was situated right on the beach, just about one and a half kilometres away from Dwarkadheesh temple. The view was beautiful from there. The sunset view-point was just hundred metres away. They all enjoyed the setting sun in the Arabian Sea. It was a breathtaking view. They got to experience the divinity of the moment.

As they walked back, fresh aroma of Khichdi was entering in their olfactory lobes. They all felt hungry and tired. Suddenly they realized how hectic their schedule had been for the entire day. Adi said, 'I have heard of the famous khichdi and osaman.' They entered inside an ordinary restaurant by the road-side. After the food was served, Anjan took a sip of hot osaman and closed his eyes, 'This is delicious. This tastes so different from the normal curry we generally eat. It is thinner and spicier, and the flavour is really good.' Virat pinched him in a mischievous tone, 'You can add some extra sliced onion with chopped tomato and chilli chutney if you want to savour it.' Anjan ordered some more items from the menu. The waiter, while serving, told them that this combo of Osaman and Khichdi was the signature dish of that locality. It was specially cooked by a particular community, called the Googly Brahmins, and was unique for its preparation. After they completed their food, the waiter brought some buttermilk, as this was necessary to help in digestion of spices, in particular. They all had a very pleasant dinner and planned to return to their hotel.

Farah said almost in a nagging voice, 'I would love to take some *Badhnis*. We have to visit the market before returning to hotel.'

'What is that?', Anjan raised his brows.

Virat explained, 'This is a special handicraft garment made by the locals of Gujarat and also in some parts of Rajasthan. The cloth is treated with a special tie and dye procedure, soaked in beautiful colours, and left to dry. The particular knotting of the clothes gives it a unique design as an end product.'

Farah was surprised with his detailing, and appreciated him, cheeringly. Maya supported Farah and off they went to shop. They all explored the local market. Maya and Farah both took some Badhni salwar suits with colourful dupattas. Farah was startled when Virat helped her select a particular pink and blue silk dress combo, about which she was unsure as there were so many beautiful options available in the shop.

The team spent the whole day like normal tourists. It was quite refreshing for all of them. After all, great ideas are borne of a calm, stable and focused mind.

After His Death

The news of civil war spread like wildfire. Yudhisthira, now being the Chakravarty Emperor of the entire Aryavarta, decided to send his most able brother to oversee the situation at Dwarka.

Arjuna bowed before Basudeva and said, 'O dear Uncle, allow me to serve you. From now on, the people of your kingdom are like my children'. He was totally shattered from inside to see the devastation caused by the rivalry and chaos within the Yadavas. The military was destroyed, most of the generals were killed. Some of them who managed to save their lives fled to far-away lands beyond the borders of Aryavarta, or went away in disguise towards the far west. There was almost no male citizen alive between the ages of twelve to sixty. There was no one to assure the safety and security of the widows, the children and the aged.

Basudeva nodded in consent and agreed. There was no option open to preserve the sovereignty of Dwarka. If the kingdom becomes a vassal state of the Pandava-ruled Hastinapur, it would get a good administrator who could look after the citizens of the kingdom. This was the need of the hour, as that would strengthen the kingdom and secure its subjects.

The wise old man held his nephew's hand, and said, 'O Partha, I have something important to tell you'. He led Arjuna to a private chamber which was secretly built in one corner of the palace. He took Arjuna to the royal treasury. This was the place where the royals had stored all the wealth as taxes collected from citizens of Dwarka. On one side of the room, there was a hidden door. He asked Arjuna to enter through the door. Then, he brought out a wooden box with beautiful engravings all over it.

The box was of moderate size, but was too heavy for the old man. The latch of the box was missing. Two semi-circular discs replaced the latch and appeared like a Chakra when the lid was closed. Two similar bejewelled chakras were present on either sides of the box. A lotus motif was carved centrally on the front and the back side of the box. Two koumaduki mace motifs lay on both sides of the lotus. A small conch was present on each of the vertical sides of the lid. Rubies and sapphires adorned the borders of the wooden box.

He struggled with his fragile hands and asked his nephew to hold it. Basudeva said, 'Please keep this safe. Protect it with everything you can. Pledge yourself before me,' he was emotional. Arjuna vowed to keep it secure and hidden beyond the reach and realm of ordinary men. He was sworn to secrecy. He knew the consequences of his failure. Basudeva added, 'You must preserve the box. Krishna would have entrusted no one but you. It should not fall into the wrong hands. Only a Worthy One can wield its power.'

Chapter Ten

ANCIENT EVIDENCES

The team met at the breakfast table the next morning.

Maya started as she was reminiscing her mother's words, '*Homo sapiens* were gradually distancing themselves from its closest animal ancestor, chimpanzees some 5 million years back. As their brain capacity increased, they became intelligent and more humane. During the earliest days, at the dawn of civilization, these beings became more organized, consciousness developed. They were bewildered by mother earth --- beauty and tranquility on one hand equated with ruthless destruction on the other. They, however, could not apprehend all that was happening around them.'

She brought out her pen and started scribbling something on her notebook. When she was finished, she showed it to the others, which read as below:-

Ignorance → Enthusiasm → Knowledge → Experience → Gratitude → Faith → Devotion --- positive path to worship

Ignorance → Apathy → Diffidence → Incompetence → Fear → Superstition --- negative path to worship

'There's always an alternative path. We choose the direction.'

They were thoroughly studying and analysing the background when Adi pointed, 'What can be the possible motives of these invasions? Why would someone repeatedly invade a specific place?'. They were discussing foreign invasions that the country went through from the early medieval period. Fascinatingly, they all agreed, the attacks might be veiled to acquire the ultimate wisdom which spread far and wide outside of India. While enjoying their morning snacks, they categorically discussed about the chronological incidents that happened across the length and breadth of the subcontinent, while trying to relate each invasion with a prehistoric and a protohistoric episode that was interlinked.

MATHURA

Vajranabha built a beautiful temple to commemorate the birthplace of his great-grandfather Krishna. Eons later, Chandragupta Vikramaditya rebuilt the temple.

Mahmud of Ghazni, on his quest for plunder, arrived near Mahaban and started ransacking the neighbouring temples. On witnessing the architectural marvel of this grand temple, he was mesmerized. Only angels could construct such a huge and magnificent structure, he wondered. He imagined how many millions of *dinars* might have been spent to build that enormous building. Even if the most skilled and experienced sculptors were employed to construct such a building, it would take over a couple of hundred years to accomplish the task. After plundering the temple, he ordered his soldiers to burn down the temple complex along with other buildings in the adjoining areas. The idols were made of gold and silver, adorned with precious gemstones. It was a mammoth job to carry tonnes of plundered wealth on hundreds of camels.

Jajja, a local confidant of the Gahadaval king Vijaypala Dev, tried rebuilding the temple by 1150 AD. People commented that the monument he built was no lesser than the earlier one, with the *shikhars* of the white temple touching the sky.

Sikandar Lodi, after becoming the Sultan of Delhi, declared that no pagans would be allowed to worship in the temple. He even banned ritualistic bathing and other religious practices on the banks of holy Yamuna river.

Jahangir was disliked by his own father. He faced violent resistance during his ascension to the throne. After becoming the emperor, he did not forget the support of his ally and granted him a favour in return. It was during his reign that Raja Veer Singh Deva Bundela, Jahangir's friend, renovated and beautified the old temple with a hefty sum in 1618 AD. Even, Prince Dara Sikoh was fond of this exquisite structure and donated a substantial amount for its beautification. But his brother Aurangzeb, who later became the emperor of Hindustan, considered the Hindu subjects as infidels. In 1669 AD, Aurangzeb ordered Abdul Nabi Khan to build Jama mosque on the ruins of Hindu temples of that area. Nabi Khan was murdered by the local Jats. This enraged Aurangzeb. The emperor himself reached to raze the Keshavdeva temple on the following winter, and constructed Eidgah, the Shahi mosque on the land of ruins. His fanatical cruelty knew no bounds. He carried away the bejewelled deities to Agra to build steps for Jahanara's mosque, so that his followers could tread on them while climbing the stairs. He also renamed Mathura as Islamabad.

VARANASI

Shiva was preaching some sermons to His beloved *Parvati*. Mata *Parvati* was feeling thirsty. Shiva dug a hole in the ground with His *Trishul* to quench her thirst. Ganga was residing then in *Brahma*'s *Kamandalu*. She was yet to descend on earth. After His preaching was over, they proceeded towards Kailash. A well was built later by His devotees. Followers of the Lord used the same water to worship. After ages, King Vikamaditya built a magnificent temple in memory of the Lord at that very same place. People remembered the significance of the place as Pragya Sarobar, the well of knowledge.

Jay Chandra, the King of Kannauj, was defeated and killed by Qutubuddin Aibak, the new Viceroy of Delhi and a Governor under the Ghurids, in 1194, in the battle of Asani. Aibak proceeded towards Kashi, the epicentre of Hindustan, and demolished more than a thousand temples, the most important of them being the Vishwanath temple of Pragya Sarobar. He built the Razia mosque in its place in a hurry, using the broken pieces of the temple as building materials, leaving many sections unaltered. After about a century, during the rule of Iltutmish, a merchant from far away Gujarat rebuilt the temple in 1230 AD and dedicated it to Avimukteshwara, to conceal the original identity of the Lord, but in vain. The news of reconstructing a temple reached Delhi. This was not accepted as a good gesture by Sikandar Lodi, and he ordered for demolition of the temple in 1447 AD. Raja Man Singh, the major general in Akbar's court built the temple once again from scratches, which got renovated under the patronage of Raja Todar Mall in 1585 AD.

The local zamindars were trying to form a united opposition against the tyrant Mughal emperor. To add to the fuel, the Brahmins started interfering with the Muslim preachers and upheld the true meaning of the *Sanatan Dharma* in this sacred land. In order to subdue this socio-political uprising, on September, 1669, Aurangzeb attacked the centre of the unrest and demolished the temple. On the fateful night of the attack, the Brahmin priests took out the main lingam and hid it in the temple well, never to be found again. The emperor built a beautiful building in its place, the architecture of which was inspired by the Taj Mahal built by his own father. He used the plinth of the temple to serve as a courtyard for the mosque. He also kept many structures unaltered. He was overwhelmed with his religious zealotry, and named it Alamgiri Mosque in memory of himself. The common people, however, as a practice, called it Pragya Sarobar.

Rani Ahilyabai Holker built a new temple to the south, on the adjoining Hill of Vishwanath. She built a seven-feet-high statue of *Nandi* and placed him at one hundred and eighty degrees from the idol inside. This was quite rare. The queen knew that the sacred bull was facing his original Lord.

SIDDHPUR

Kardama, the great sage and son of Lord *Brahma*, sat on the banks of the sacred Saraswati river, and started his meditation in search of the eternal truth. Times flew by, but the sage was immersed in his penance. Seeing his dedication, Lord Vishnu was highly moved and tears came out of His eyes, which accumulated to form a pond. Eons later, this waterbody would become one of the five most sacred bathing places on earth, in the name of Bindu Sarovar. The Lord graced him with His presence and granted him a blissful Garhastya life. Soon after, the sage was married to the beautiful Devahuti. They had nine daughters, who in turn became mothers of great sages. He was also blessed with a son as graceful as the Lord Himself. When his son was born, he named him Kapila. Kardama denounced his family after a short while, to spend the rest of his life as an ascetic.

Kapila, in turn, became a pious and highly revered person, and took over his father's place in the *ashrama*. One day, at his mother's request, he explained his mystical and devotional realization in the form of *Sankhya Yoga*. Having delivered the highest knowledge to his mother and other attendees of the ashrama, he followed his father to Bindu Sarovar. Devahuti, in turn, after realising the supreme spirituality in herself, left the material world and transformed into sacred Gyanvapi river, where demi-gods and people would come for a sanctimonious bath.

Lord Parshuram, after killing His mother, Devi Renuka, reached the banks of Saraswati river. He was in deep remorse after the incident, and paid His last respect to His beloved mother on the banks of the river.

Ever since, the place became pious and holy in the name of Sristhala. It became the only place on earth to perform the *matru-shradh*, a ritual service for the salvation of one's deceased mother, and offer *pinda*, like Gaya where people performed last rites of forefathers. Departed souls were revered and remembered through *mantras* and *yajnas*.

Five *swayambhu* Shivalingas were being worshipped by local people from ages. They emerged naturally. Mularaja, who founded the Chalukya dynasty, heard this story of the Shivalingas from his childhood. He was himself a great devotee of Shiva. He upheld the significance of the place, and started constructing a temple in the name of Lord Rudra in 943 AD. He however could not witness the completed temple in his lifetime. The temple was given final shape by his successor Jayasimha Siddharaja in 1140 AD. It was a massive structure with over a thousand pillars, double the number of idols and flags, and intricately carved ornate entrances. Siddharaja invited one thousand Udichya Brahmins, who carried and practised the knowledge of the Vedas, and gifted them seven hundred villages to reside. They consecrated the Lord in the temple and continued the tradition. The king established his capital there and christened the place in his name, Siddhpur.

Mohammed Ghori heard of the enormous wealth plundered by Mahmud of Ghazni from the Somnath temple and decided to attack. On his way to Somnath in 1197 AD, he reached at Rudra Mahalaya temple in Siddhpur, another Shiva temple, like the one at Somnath. He was amazed at the splendour of the temple. He looted, desecrated the

Lingam, and destroyed parts of it. The temple was again attacked and destroyed by Ulugh Khan and Nusrat Khan, the generals of Alauddin Khalji in 1296-1299 AD. Later, during the rule of Ahmed Shah I, the temple was demolished in 1415 AD, and Jami Masjid, a congregational mosque was built in its place. When Akbar ascended the throne in the 15th Century, Siddhpur came under the Mughal empire. By this time, the temple collapsed, and became a ruin. Aurangzeb restored and beautified the mosque on the ruins of the temple.

MODHERA SUN TEMPLE, GUJARAT

Lord Rama was deeply aggrieved after killing the great Brahmin Ravana. He was filled with remorse. He wanted to absolve Himself of the great sin of *Brahmahatya*. Guru Vashistha advised Him to perform a yagna in Dharmaranya, the forest of righteousness. He was assisted by the Modha Brahmins, the locals residing in Modherak village. He followed all the instructions by his Guru while performing the yagna on the banks of river Pushpavathi, and returned to Ayodhya. The yagna pit, where the Lord performed the rituals then was reminisced by the locals as Rama Kund.

After pillaging Somnath temple, Mahmud accumulated bounty of wealth. He slaughtered the local people and destroyed everything. On his return journey, he came to Modhera, where there was a small temple around the Rama Kund. Curious to know what was inside the temple, he tried to enter. He was surprised at the fierce resistance put across by the unarmed villagers. Being certain that there was nothing to loot in Rama Kund, he abandoned his hunt and left the place.

King Bheemadeva, being jubilant at the courage of his people for defending the temple, began constructing a monumental shrine in memory of his *Kuladevata*, the Sun God in 1026 AD.

Alauddin Khilji came to know of the Sun Temple while on his conquest of Gujarat. He marched in his grand style, as he had done before while attacking and plundering many other Hindu temples, and carried away the main idol from the Sun Temple.

MARTAND SUN TEMPLE, KASHMIR

In the north, there was a beautiful land called Rishibhumi. Sage Kashyap told his son, 'You are now the protector of this sacred land, fed by the waters of Vitasta, and marked by this lake Satisara. O Neel, make this land as shiny, prosperous and glittering as the Sun itself.'

Sage Neel, entrusted with the great duty, dedicated his kingdom to Martand, the Sun God. He built a grand Sun Temple on the plateau overseeing the whole of Kashmir Valley. The structure had eighty-four columns indicating each of the seven days of the Sun God and his celestial journey across the twelve Rashis.

The Nagas from Karkot empire and the Garudas of the Suparna empire in Gandhara differed ideologically and often engaged in war. But they had one thing in common – both clans were great devotees of the Sun God. This temple was a common string for them.

The descriptions of this heavenly place spreaded far and wide. The Sufi preacher Mir Muhammad Hamadani advised King Sikandar Shah Miri to acquire detailed informations about Kashmir Valley. The King was on a spree for treasure-hunt, and this was one of the main temples dedicated to the God associated with the treasure he was looking for.

Miri attacked the temple of the *Kafers* and removed all the idols. But he did not find the hidden treasure. The king, in despair, ordered the demolition of the entire temple complex.

HAMPI

Pampa was the dearest daughter of *Brahma*. When she grew up, she envisioned herself to be a partner of her beloved *Shiva*. She left her home and went to a forest to meditate. Seeing her penance, *Kamdev* tried to assist her by waking the Lord from His *samadhi*. *Shiva* fumed at his desperation, and burned him alive. When He came to know the reason for poor Kamdev's advent, He went to the forest to validate Pampa's faith. He tried his best to dissuade her beliefs, but Pampa was deeply in love with the Lord. Seeing her dedication, Shiva agreed to marry her.

The monkey prince was heavily panting as he stood before Sage Matanga. Earlier in the day, he had a fierce combat with the King of Kishkindha. He had to flee from his own brother, the great Vali, to save his life. The sage took him under his protection and assured him safety on that hilltop. He prophesied that no one would ever be able to cross the Tungabhadra and ascend Hemakuta hill with an evil intent. Later, Sugriva would be rescued by Lord Vishnu, in His supreme Avatar at the appropriate time. Advent of Lord would restore peace and stability in that land. The kingdom established after Lord's arrival was peaceful, and became one of the main centres of religion, culture and architecture under the able leaderships of rulers for centuries.

From the time of Ashoka the Great, till the rule of the Chalukyas in the tenth Century, and then under the Hoysalas from the twelfth to fourteenth century, many beautiful temples were built in memory of several Hindu deities. The main temple was the Virupaksha temple, dedicated to Lord Shiva, which became the centre for knowledge in the region.

The first ruler to reach this place from northern India was Alauddin Khalji, in the late thirteenth Century. He was on a mission to expand the Muslim Sultanate. In 1326 AD, Muhammad bin Tughlaq, the Delhi Sultan, invaded Kampili kingdom in search of his unfaithful general, Baha-Ud-Din Gurshtasp. The rebellious general had taken refuge in the court of Pratap Rudra. Tughlaq destroyed most of the temples, massacred the common people, and left with his war booty.

About ten years later, two brothers Harihara I and Bukka I, both commanders of Hoysala empire, were entrusted with the duty of warding off the Muslim invaders from North India. They established the Vijaynagara empire in 1336 AD from the ruins of Kakatiya kingdom under the guidance and blessings of the twelfth *Jagadguru*, sage Vidyaranya. Under their patronage, the kingdom flourished, infrastructure and intellectual developments reached the pinnacle. People from distant lands of Persia and Portugal developed trade relations, and were attracted towards south India. In about a century, it became the richest kingdom of India under Krishna Deva Raya. Under his rule, the boundaries touched the seas in three directions. On the fateful day of 23rd January, 1565, a huge coalition army of Muslim sultanates gathered at Talikota on the banks of the mighty Krishna river, and attacked Vijayanagara. The attack was borne of religious bigotry. The strong army of King Aliya Rama Raya was on the verge of winning, when suddenly two Muslim generals switched sides and aided the coalition. The army was confused by this frenzy of treacherous act, and taking advantage of this situation, the king was captured and beheaded. The invaders then destroyed all the architectures – both at civil and religious places – and plundered all the wealth. It took almost six months for them to burn the beautiful metropolitan, and turn it into ruins. They however could not do any major harm to the grand Virupaksha temple. It is believed that the temple on the Hemakut hill was protected by a boon from ancient times. The invaders however showed much interest in plundering and burning the Balakrishna temple on the other side of the hill. They also attacked the double shrine of *Shiva* and *Vishnu*. The large ten feet high monolithic *Shiva Linga*, half submerged in water, was spared, while they destroyed the twenty-two feet high Yoga Narasimha statue, dismembered the beautiful statue of Goddess Lakshmi, and put fire to the pedestal. These burnt marks are visible even today.

AYODHYA

The young man disguised himself as a Sufi ascetic, and started his journey from Kabul. He was on a mission of collecting information on the trend of various warlords who were keen on acquiring the land beyond the Indus. After several months, he reached Awadh and met two great saints of that time, who blessed him to become the master of the land he had travelled. They told him that this was his destiny. He took their blessings and pledged to be successful on his expedition.

On his return journey, he met Sikandar Lodhi, the Turco-Afghan ruler of the Delhi Sultanate. He realized that if there was anyone who could jeopardise his mission, it was Lodhi.

Following his return to his homeland, he prepared himself for a war in Hindustan. He also got support from the Caliphate with ingenious and modern weaponry. After taking control of Delhi, he came back to the place from where he started. In order to fulfil his pledge to the saints, he built a grand mosque upon the ruins of a temple. This temple was believed to be the birthplace of ever-venerated and most prominent avatar of Lord Vishnu.

History remembered him as Babur Qalandar, and he paved the way for the establishment of a major dynasty this land had ever seen. His able successors accomplished in building a strong empire for the next few centuries till the arrival of the White Moghuls.

VRINDAVAN

The thirteen-year-old boy was curious about the appearance of Lord Krishna. After all, the answer he was seeking was quite valid, as he was carrying the lineage and the Lord was none other than his own great-grandfather. He kept asking this question to his grandmother Rukmavati, whom he liked the most. He was confident that she must have had the answer. She was the daughter-in-law of the Lord, and surely had observed Him well. He however was unaware of the tradition women followed those days. A direct eye contact between a daughter-in-law and father-in-law was treated as disrespect and hence prohibited . But the boy was right; she could not miss the opportunity of glancing at Him once. She had been worshipping Lord Krishna all her life. Assured of this, the boy started building an idol of the Lord which would help the future generations to remember the face of the Lord, as his grandmother had described. When it was completed, he brought the idol before her in joy and excitement. But to his disappointment, she said that it resembled the lower portion, of the Lord, from navel to the lotus feet. The boy however preserved the idol and named it Madan Mohan Ji.

The boy started carving again. After finishing the second one, he brought his grandmother to examine the idol. She said that it resembled the upper body, of the Lord, from the navel to the neck, the chest and the arms. The boy did not lose his hope, and kept the idol with him under the name of Gopi Nath Ji.

On his third attempt, the boy was meticulous to build an idol as perfect as he could. This time, his hard work yielded results. When he showed it to her, she burst into tears of joy. The idol ideally represented His face, large forehead and big eyes. Elated, the boy named it Shri Govind Dev Ji, and preserved all the three idols he had built.

Several years later, he was coronated as the king of Mathura by Parikshit, the grandson of Arjuna. The new king built three separate temples to enshrine the three idols he built in his childhood. Now the people of the land had the opportunity to behold the beauty of the Lord in their own eyes. The king however, unknowingly, divided the Lord into three parts, never to be united again.

As time passed by, the temples were abandoned and people forgot all the richness of their past. The mighty had fallen, the place had literally turned into a jungle. Unable to maintain it further, the priests hid the idols under a banyan tree, leaving some clues behind for mankind.

Many centuries later, Vishvambar Mishra, an ardent follower of Lord Krishna, and proponent of Bhakti Yoga, undertook a mission to rediscover Vrindavan, the place where the Lord had spent His transcendent pastimes. By then, the young man was enlightened with the ultimate consciousness, the *Chetana* of the Lord, and came to be known as Chaitanya. In 1514 AD, he left his native place Nabadwip in Bengal to restore the areas which were rich with the memories of his Lord. He was a great scholar of ancient Indian scriptures. He discovered the *Sapta Devalaya*, the seven main temples as described in the *Bhagawat Purana*. But he could not find the three main idols. Disheartened, he went to spend the remaining days of his life at Puri.

It was more than a year that he was residing in Puri. One night, he envisioned the exact location of the idols and the temples associated with them, while he was meditating. He immediately asked his two disciples to go there and unearth the idols. The Goswami brothers obeyed their Guru and were successful in their mission at the holy land. With limited resources and a meagre fund, they managed to build three temples and enshrined the idols again.

The priests received the news of the advent of an emperor, a ruthless zealot. Aurangzeb had already invaded the holy city of Varanasi, and was planning an attack on Mathura, Vrindavan and adjoining areas with a religious vendetta in mind. They took no risk and hid the three main idols inside a well. One night, King Gopal Singh had a weird dream when Lord Krishna instructed him to take away the idols from Vrindavan to Rajasthan in the darkness of the night. The king obeyed the orders, and established great temples in his homeland. He enshrined Sri Madan Mohan Ji at Karoli, while Sri Gopi Nath Ji and Sri Govind Dev Ji were placed in temples at Jaipur.

The emperor attacked the temples, the largest and grandest among them was that of Sri Madan Mohan Ji, in 1670 AD. When thousands of lamps were lit in that seven-storied architecture, people could see the lights from far away. He was shocked when he could not see anything inside. Enraged, he ordered to demolish the top four stories of the temple.

JAGANNATHA TEMPLE, PURI

There were several mysteries associated with the Jagannatha Temple at Puri. No one knew with certainty who was the original builder of the temple, or why the idols were sculpted in that peculiar form, though many folklores hovered around the corner. Whoever came to this place witnessed some surprising facts by themselves. Among many, few facts were: the sound of the gushing winds from the sea and that of waves hitting the shoreline disappeared once any devotee put their first step inside the temple through the Lion Gate; the shadow of the dome of sixty-five metre tall building was never visible at any point of the day; the flag atop the temple always flew in the opposite direction of the wind; not a single bird ever dared to fly over the temple; the food cooked inside the largest kitchen in the world was never exhausted nor wasted; food was prepared first in the topmost earthen cooking pot though the fire was at the base; the secret source of sweet water inside the kitchen in spite of the temple being situated on a sea beach. However, the fact that the devotees were allowed to worship their Lord after having a sumptuous meal attracted a large section of followers. It was believed that an empty stomach would always distract them away from the Lord towards meeting their own basic needs.

In spite of undergoing numerous assaults, which was common with many such places of worship, each time the temple recovered and rose back to its earlier grandeur even better than before. The most remarkable attacks on the Jagannatha Temple in Puri however could be listed as following,

- Plunder of the temple by Raktavahu in the ninth century AD, though the agenda was more of a political rather than a religious one or a treasure hunt
- Second Invasion by Illias Shah who was the Sultan of Bengal
- By Feroze Shah Tughlaq in 1360 AD
- By Ismail Ghazi who was the commander of Allauddin Hussain Shah, Sultan of Bengal, in 1509 AD
- By Kalapahara in 1568 AD, the fifth attack
- By Suleman and Osman. Suleman was the son of Kuthu Shah whereas Osman was the son of Isha, the ruler of Odisha
- By Mirza Khurrum, the commander of Islam Khan who was the Nawab of Bengal, in 1601 AD
- By Hasim Khan in 1608 AD. He was the Subedar of Odisha
- By Kesodasmaru who was a *jagirdar* and a Hindu Rajput
- By Kalyan Malla, son of Raja Todar Mall, in 1611 AD, the tenth attack on the temple
- By Kalyan Malla again in 1612 AD
- By Mukarram Khan in 1617AD
- By Mirza Ahmad Beg who was the nephew of Nurjahan, wife of Jahangir
- By Amir Mutaquad Khan in 1641 AD
- By Amir Fateh Khan in 1647 AD
- By Ekram Khan, the Nawab of Odisha, in 1699 AD
- By Muhammad Taqi Khan in 1731 AD
- By the followers of Alekh religion in 1881 AD, the eighteenth and the last one, after which the British acted as the protector of the shrine under their rule

Every invasion in our motherland was primarily targeted to destroy, plunder and wreak havoc. Countless lives were taken to instil fear and subjugate masses. The intention behind these attacks was not only military dominance but also to tear down the faith and belief of the local people. The invaders knew that, it was necessary to wield the military power to crush an enemy. But to vanquish the opponent, it was necessary to obliterate the knowledge and belief system of the population in general so that they could be subjugated to slavery. The temples were epicentre of knowledge, seat of ancient wisdom, and this was the actual power craved by mortals. In addition, the temples were built lavishly, thousands of craftsmen were employed to make it even more exquisite in comparison to other contemporary monuments. They also contained huge amount of wealth thereby becoming centre of attraction. The plunderers tried to control the subcontinent by categorically annihilating the actual power, be it in the temples or other monuments. The act was reflected when Takshashila, Vikramshila and Nalanda universities, centres of excellence in terms of every aspect of science and literature, were razed to ground. Pupils from all over the world came to these universities to study and research. Destruction of temples were substantiated by repeated invasions at Somnath, Mathura, Varanasi, Siddhpur, Modhera Sun Temple (Gujarat), Martand Sun Temple (Kashmir), Hampi, Ayodhya, Vrindavan, Jagannatha Temple (Puri), to name a few.

'We all are bewildered with the Fibonacci series,' Maya reminded as everyone present in the audience could easily recollect one of the most famous mathematical series of numbers she was referring to. 'It is the most beautiful series which is even represented in nature in many ways like the distribution of petals of a flower, the growth of seeds, and many such things. But there is a hidden story behind this. It is generally accepted to be discovered by the Italian mathematician Leonardo Bonacci in 1200 AD. He was greatly inspired by the Jain saint Hemachandra, who explained him how to compose poems in eight *matras*. After his return from India, he wrote a book named *Liber Abacci*. He was disgusted with the use of Abacus for counting during those days in his homeland, and remembered how the Indians could count upto billions effortlessly. He described the procedure in a chapter named *Modus Indorum* – Method of Indians. Later historians described the meaning of his book as *Liber* for Library, and *Abacci* for Abacus, thus *Liber Abacci* became Book of Calculation. But many historians alternatively believe that *Liber* meant Liberation and *Abacci* meant Abacus, and so *Liber Abacci* meant Liberation from Calculation using Abacus.'

Virat said in a heavy voice, 'Yes, the original father of arithmetic was Brahmagupta, who had described easy steps for addition, subtraction, multiplication and division in 600 AD. Before that, in around 200 BC, Pingala described the use of metres, an arithmetic method for the composition of shlokas and poems in his book *Chhandasashtra*. The difference is, while the West documented all their discoveries efficiently and used patents to safeguard and exercise control, our ancient knowledge was passed on verbally from Gurus to disciples, for generations, without attracting the outside world for showcasing their feat.'

All of them reminisced about the rich heritage and scientific advancements in every aspect of human knowledge in ancient and medieval India. From arts to architecture and *Vaastu Shastra* (Science of architecture), from astronomy to astrology, from the knowledge of the heliocentric *Souro Mondal* (Solar system) to the existence of *Nava Graha* (nine planets), from the round shape of the

Earth, as depicted in the *Varaha Avatar* (third incarnation of Lord Vishnu) holding the *Bhudevi* (Mother Earth Goddess) in His tusks to medicines capable of healing almost every ailment in *Ayurveda* to the operative procedures and plastic surgeries by Dhanvantari and in the *Sushruta Samhita*, from *Vaimanik Shatra* (knowledge and models of building aircrafts) to *Gurutwa-akarshan* (knowledge of gravitational force), the list goes on. They considered themselves fortunate enough to be engaged in a mission which would give them a chance to uphold the hidden knowledge from the past and discover and redesign one of the most powerful weapon that ever existed and used on this planet.

Beginning of the End

Arjuna reached Indraprastha with a heavy heart and narrated all incidents to his family. He talked about the civil war that transpired subsequently and consumed whole of Dwarka. But he intentionally skipped the secret conversation he had with Basudeva. Listening to his account, Yudhisthira decided that it was time for them to denounce this mundane world. All the brothers, along with queen Draupadi left Indraprastha and sought refuge in the Himalayas. They entered into the penultimate phase of Aryan life cycle, called Banaprastha.

Yudhisthira coronated Parikshit as the King of Hastinapur. Vajranabha, the great-grandson of Krishna, was selected as the king of Mathura in memory of their beloved friend.

The five brothers along with Draupadi set out for a pilgrimage towards the east. At first, they were not sure about their destination. They wanted to spend their final days in penance. Arjuna and Bheema both pinned down Meru Parvat as their final destination. This was the peak which played significant role in the past, and many Holy deeds were associated with it. But, the Head of the family had something different brewing in his mind. He carefully observed each one's belongings and pondered about the individual goal and lifelong struggle of each member of his family, and the karmic results gained through those deeds. Finally, he shared his thoughts, and all the brothers, and Draupadi, agreed gladly. How could they ignore the opportunity to live their final days in such a place! A heavenly abode, which was desired by every human being on earth!

Chapter Eleven

TECHNICAL DISCUSSIONS

They decided to remain at the hotel, and brainstorm on the project. They had travelled and collected much information about the life of Lord Krishna. It was now time to concentrate on the subject.

After having had their breakfast at the hotel cafeteria, they all assembled at Adi's room to discuss in detail.

Farah said, 'I used to visualize *Brahmastra* as some kind of a nuclear bomb, a powerful weapon of mass destruction. But now I think that it must be a projectile which can be activated by *mantras*, some kind of voice command and password or passphrase, and can be aimed at a specific target.'

Anjan exclaimed, 'Why? We have read in Mahabharata that it had a similar destructive capacity as an atomic bomb. We get similar stories regarding this.' He was referring to some quotes that were readily available in popular search engines on the internet which described the use of atomic weapons in ancient India.

Farha explained, 'See, we have read that the *Brahmastra* projected by Aswatthama was directed at Uttara's womb to kill the unborn baby Parikshit. Any nuke will cause some collateral damage. So, it was a highly precise remotely guided projectile.'

'The *Chakra*', Maya said, 'was a spinning disc-like weapon that had ten million spikes on two rows that moved in opposite directions. It returned to Krishna's or *Vishnu's* right index finger every time after accomplishing its designated task.'

Anjan was playing the Devil's advocate. He interjected, 'If it is true that ancient India had so much technological advancements to build such sophisticated weapons, why no one else in the world know anything about this?'

Farah added, 'Technology was indeed much advanced in the times of Mahabharata. Sanjay, the driver of Dhritrashtra, had a remote audio-visual system, just like the modern day television. The Kauravas were none other than one hundred test tube babies. They also had missiles and anti-missiles that they used abundantly in warfare.'

Virat jumped in, 'See, we have only single use missiles as of now. But SpaceX is experimenting with such a rocket which will be able to return to earth after being launched into space. It will be of multiple use. The question arises that, if a missile hits a target, then how can it return to its launch pad? The solution to this is MIRV, Multiple Independently targetable Re-entry Vehicle. It consists of multiple small missiles. These missiles hit multiple targets, while the carrier missile can be re-used multiple times. But, till now no one has envisaged a disc-like MIRV. There might be some hindrances towards designing such a compact, effective, multi-usable weapon.'

Adi reminded him, 'Hey, we are already on this project. The final outcome of our research is to design such a weapon only.'

Farah continued, 'Another weapon that is mentioned is the *Vaishnavastra* – it used to hit the target with tremendous speed. It was the fastest weapon in Mahabharata war. It was not released towards the target, but upwards. After that, it hit the target from above with tremendous speed. It released dangerous fires. We have a weapon parallel to this, we have the *Brahmos* with us, the fastest cruise missile. Some missiles are released vertically upwards towards space, goes out of the atmosphere, and then returns and hits the target from above much like fire. Our country has already developed the Sourya Missile, which has achieved a speed of Mach7. Research is ongoing to develop missiles faster than this.'

Anjan tried to summarize the discussions. He imagined and said, 'Maybe the Sudarshan Chakra moved in a circular fashion so that it could get the lift, and could keep itself stable. The material with which it was built was unique in nature. It was stronger than diamond, as it could cut any material. It revolved and made itself so stable so that it could be balanced on a single finger. Now, the question is how the Chakra was controlled and how the target was defined. I think there must be a receiver in the Chakra which was synchronized with the brain-wave of Krishna, and could interpret the thoughts that were there in His mind. This was almost conceptualised by the great scientist Tesla, the famous five megahertz wave model, but he was forced to abandon his project mid-way. This synchronization was used to command the weapon to activate and lock its target. We already have mind-controlled racing cars as toy models with emotive insights. It interprets the electrical impulses released by neurons, and activates the device. We have already become successful in creating patterns on the computer with our brain-waves. Numerous evidences are present where a machine can be controlled simply by the human brain, without the necessity of even using a remote control.'

Adi prompted, 'Yes, many countries are now researching on Sudarshan Chakra. It can be designed, but cannot be given the energy to move at such a high speed with precision. The main problem is the fuel that needs to be used in Sudarshan Chakra. It is speculated that China has already developed such a weapon, which is a cause of major contention in the West. It spins and revolves like the Sudarshan Chakra, and is made to intercept ballistic missile fired from the ground. They have already tested this weapon within their boundary. It has been designed to intercept Inter Continental Ballistic Missiles.'

The Great Ascension

*P*andavas arrived at Rishikesh. From there, they had to ascend towards the Shiwaliks, the foothills of the mighty Himalayas. After crossing Himachal, a comparatively flat region, they faced a new challenge. Though the slopes were less abrupt, the members of the family were exhausted after the long trek they undertook. Mortal age had taken a toll on their physical health. They had to cross Himadri, the mighty snow peaks, to reach the northern plains, often called the roof of the world, for its vast expanse and relatively flat terrain along the northern boundaries of the Himalayas.

They identified a mountain pass between the Sutlej and the Indus valley to cross Himadri. Though it was quite tough to trek further, they had strong will-power and determination to reach there. After all, they were proven to be the strongest in whole of Aryavarta.

Years of struggle and hardship had strengthened them from within, validated by thirteen years of exile followed by the Great War of Kurukshetra.

After crossing the Dhauladhar Mountains, they went further north and finally reached their destination.

Chapter Twelve

The Idea Behind the Weapon

Maya started noting down key points of their discussion in her official laptop. The weapon should incorporate every specifications they discussed, to render itself exceptional. Further research was necessary to reduce the gap between concepts and implementation.

The Sudarshan Chakra was a perfect example of Artificial Intelligence, Machine Learning and Robotics. It included Radio Frequency and scanning system, LIDAR (Light Detection and Ranging), Coding, and Database for identifying and locking on the target.

It could not be used on a specific target twice after the opponent surrendered. It was coded such that it could apprehend whether it was being used on surrendered enemies, so as to verify the intention of the user also. It had an inbuilt metal detecting system.

Two anti-rotating discs were used for the levitation of the weapon. The lower disc was used to deliver energy to the upper disc. There might be altering gravity due to magnetism, or may be some other technology for levitation. Also, the counter-rotating upper and lower discs provided counter torques and stability during its flight.

The power of the weapon was derived from some sort of nuclear energy, and this energy was converted to other forms, including fire.

The weapon had its own intelligence. It used to be activated by voice command.

It was a kind of mind controlled airborne craft, similar to a modern-day fidget spinner-like setup.

It was built of a material, that was tough enough to withstand the heat and power generated within. It produced harmonic directed force to tear through any weapon in close combat.

It was a hand-held nuclear device, which could spin for a very long time with ultra-high speed, and the nuclear energy made it a devastating weapon with an almost un-exhaustible source of power.

It was much like a miniature Direct Energy Weapon, as it countered and destroyed all other weapons of varying shapes and sizes.

However, they noticed something peculiar about the weapon. It was capable to deter any incoming weapon from the opponent, all of which became incapacitated, without any physical contact. Also, the more resistance it faced from the approaching target, the more powerful it became. It seemed to suck the power from the very shield which was trying to deter the Chakra.

Maya said, 'All these indicates that the Chakra had two exceptional qualities: disabling weapons from a distance as well as ability to destroy armament in close combat. Isn't it indicating a very familiar technology of the present? Many countries, including India have already developed some weapons using this technology, though there is much scope for improvement in the future. I am talking about the Direct Energy Weapons. These are very precise with limited collateral damage, and so this technology has become a preferred mechanism for futuristic weapons.'

Everybody cheered as Maya hit the bull's eye. They all decided to research further by delving deeper into the topic, and use this technology as the basic offensive mechanism for their proposed prototype.

It was time for lunch. They decided that they would not opt for room service. Something was brewing in Adi's mind. It was obvious that the notes about their discussion points, scribbles and sketches, and any related clues were lying scattered in their room. They all went to the restaurant and ordered their food, like other tourists who gathered at the hotel for a leisure trip. They, however, did not discuss anything related to their project there. After a heavy lunch, they all proceeded to Adi's room. A waiter approached Adi abruptly with a tray. There was a bill lying on the tray, which needed to be signed. There was something else too. Adi signed the food bill as he quickly glanced at the white envelope. Adi and Anjan looked at each other. The waiter handed over the envelope to Adi, and returned with a smile. Adi frowned, and opened the envelope with apprehension. He found a folded white paper, but surprisingly the paper was blank. Adi asked the others to return. Anjan stayed back. Both of them looked worried. This time Adi could not neglect it.

Back in Adi's room, they decided to study and accumulate all available information regarding every attributes of the Chakra, especially on Maya's proposition. Each member selected specific subject based on their professional expertise. They became busy in researching on their assignments for the remaining hours of the day. Data was collected from their organization archives and public websites. The team agreed to collate the information on the next day.

DEW ON THE GRASS

Adi and Farah shared the responsibility of exploring Direct Energy weapons and about the power source of such weapons.

Adi began with a story. He said, 'The earliest use of direct energies can be traced back to Greek legends. There is a popular narrative that Archimedes developed a device to burn the enemy ships by harnessing the power from the sunrays. It was a series of mirrors with adjustable focal length. But scientists have not been able to recreate such a device with the power to burn ships till date. It is however believed that a similar device could have been used to create a blinding effect so as to distract the crew of the enemy line.' He showed a picture on his tab.

Adi now began describing the Direct Energy Weapon in details. 'These weapons do not have any solid projectile. Instead, they use focussed energy of different forms in high concentration to damage the targets. Types of energies used are laser, microwave, particle beam and sound beams.'

'Research is going on to use DEW as an anti-missile defence system, and for other flight and glide vehicles. Many other countries around the world are also trying to develop such weapons. Though, they claim that most of the research are still at their initial stages of development.'

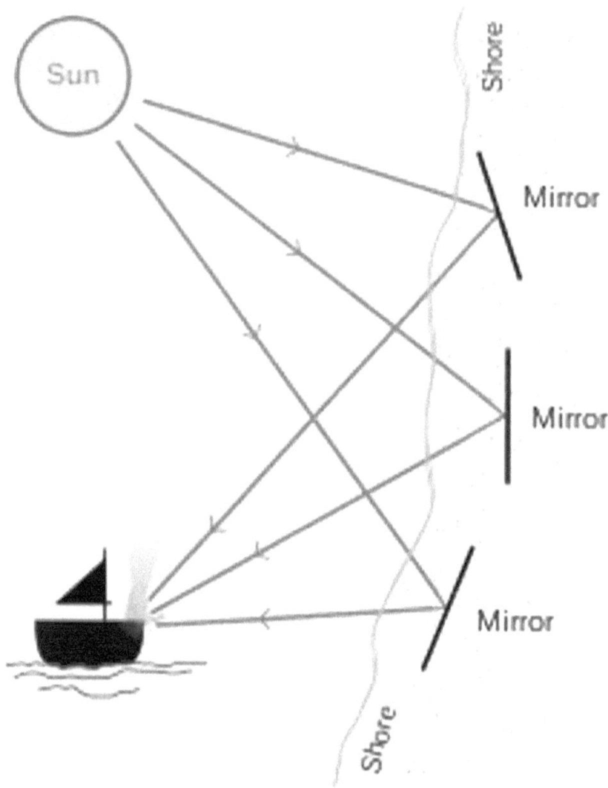

Fig. 7 : *Archimedes' heat ray: conceptual diagram (source: Wikipedia, Archimedes, https://simple.wikipedia.org/wiki/Archimedes)*

Maya said chirpily, 'I have read about a pistol used by Professor Shanku, a character created by Satyajit Ray, a vivid writer and an Oscar-winning director from Bengal. Shanku named it Annihilin Pistol. The Professor used it seldom to erase and vanish his enemy into thin air literally! The pistol had no bullets.' All her team members found the story amusing.

Adi paused, so as to arrange the contents of his analysis. He continued, 'There are many advantages of such weapons. They operate at the speed of light, much like laser and microwaves. They are not affected by common factors like gravity and wind. They are also unaffected by dispersion, absorption and scattering, and hence can have a long range. Lastly, these weapons are cheaper than conventional weapons in terms of logistics, as long as there is a steady source of power.'

He carried on, 'Some well-advertised weapons of such category are the once disputed *Active Denial System* which evaporated moisture from human skin and caused immense pain, the *Vigilant Eagle* – an airport defence system comprising of an array of fixed grid Infra-Red cameras which used to tear away the communication and control system of any incoming air-borne missile to deflect its path, *Stupor* – an Anti-Drone rifle which emitted electromagnetic pulses to destroy the navigation and communication channels of Drones, and was thought to be used extensively in the recent conflict between Russia and Ukraine. But, since directivity was a challenge during operating such weapons, it causes bilateral damage to the civilians and induces irreversible illness, some common examples of which are breathing problems, disorientation and systematic discomfort, nausea, pain and vertigo.'

'The main problem of developing such weapons was feeding adequate power to operate. They are energy mongers, and require huge amount of energy. This limitation has hindered their usage in times of war. It is difficult to deploy these weapons when needed as mostly war grounds are distant from source of power generation.' Adi stopped and approached towards the centre table to take a bottle of water.

Farah was just waiting for her turn. She came straight. 'I will directly delve into two of the most prestigious and coveted defence projects undertaken in India. From ancient times, Indians have always imagined of an ultimate source of power as their saviour from evil forces. *Shakti* always protected them and triumphed over where the most powerful Gods and warriors were defeated. They have adorably named *her* and made them their deity. In accordance, the DRDO and BARC had started their researches on a particle accelerator to convert electron energy impulses into electromagnetic radiation. This radiation can then be turned into X-Rays or microwave frequencies to destroy enemy missiles and aircrafts. They have named this as KALI, an acronym for Kilo Ampere Linear Injector.'

'The next in line is DURGA – a classified project on Directionally Unrestricted Ray-Gun Array. It has been planned to be operational from land, sea as well as air-based platforms. It is more flexible to use, and has a wide range of deployment.'

The team retired for their evening tea. This time, they opted for room service. As Maya was flipping over the pages of restaurant menu card, the doorbell rang. To their surprise, the same room service boy who was attending them from the very first day, was standing at the door with that usual smile on his face. It seemed that he was present all along, and might be eavesdropping, although he acted differently. He tried to serve in the most hospitable way. Adi, ignoring his gesture, ordered some snacks and tea for all. He asked the waiter to get the food served in their room as quickly as possible.

Destination – The First View

The whole family erupted in joy at the sight of the Golden Gates. The first rays of the Sun were shining in splendour, as they reflected from the temple tops and the adjoining buildings. The entire place dazzled, as if it was wrapped in gold. They were enamoured of the beauty that lay in front of them. It was rightfully called the abode of the Gods.

As they approached the Gates, they were stopped by the guards. One of them, who appeared to be the strongest among all, started interrogating them. He identified himself as Agni, the chief of Guard of the Land, and asked politely to help him for a physical frisking.

All the brothers had already left behind their material belongings while leaving Indraprastha. But, Arjuna was still carrying his Gandiva bow and the bejewelled wooden box he received from Basudeva. After a brief conversation and discussion, Agni told that he could not allow them to enter the place with any kind of ammunitions. A black dog was accompanying them faithfully from the far-away planes, all along. The chief of the gatekeepers frowned at the dog. As if the unwelcoming guests were not enough to create a matter of contention, the presence of a dog enraged him further. Agni could not recognize the Chakravarty emperor. Worn and exhausted from a long journey, the elderly travellers resembled nothing like the mighty Pandavas. He disapproved their right to entry and summarily rejected their requests. Yudhisthira pleaded and tried to convince him, but all his attempts of negotiation fell on deaf ears. On further appeal, Agni went inside leaving the gates under the supervision of other heavily armed custodians. He wanted to confirm his doubt and consult with his higher authorities. The guests were asked to wait outside the premises. They awaited eagerly, with the hope of getting permission to enter in their dreamland. Every moment felt like an eternity.

Chapter Thirteen

THE POWER

'And now, movie time!' Farah rejoiced as she showed a clip from the Iron Man movie.

In the famous MCU (Marvel Cinematic Universe) movie, the male billionaire protagonist was severely injured by a missile blast. Somehow he managed to escape from there, but his heart was punctured by several iron shrapnels, and he was on the verge of his death. To protect his heart from the impending shrapnels, Tony Stark created a personal arc reactor to supply power to an electromagnet which kept these shrapnels away from piercing his heart.

Farah was explaining the superior possibility of harnessing an immense amount of energy which could be generated from an arc reactor.

'Currently, generation of electricity from fusion reactors is the main focus of research all across the world. If implemented, this will be the cleanest energy source. It will be a major breakthrough in human history, like the one when humans first controlled fire.'

'In principle, the arc reactor fuses two isotopes of Hydrogen (H), viz. Deuterium($_1H^2$ or D) and Tritium ($_1H^3$or T), at high energy and a temperature of above one hundred million degree Celsius. When fusion occurs, the plasma contains Helium (He) and a free neutron, and their combined mass is lesser than that of the initial isotopes. The mass lost in the reaction is converted to energy. This energy can then be used as per requirement. While deep research is currently ongoing for the improvisation of the technology, the idea is a possibility.'

'On a lighter note', she said with her usual sense of humour, 'we can easily create plasma in our home with a microwave oven as a power source, and using some common raw materials like a matchstick, or some aluminium foils, or even with some grapes.'

All others smiled, while she continued.

'As is shown in the movie, the shape of the fusion reactor is like a donut, and was called a Tokamak. The main trick is to keep the plasma contained within the reactor. This can be done by creating a magnetic field. To sustain the high temperature, the magnetic core is made from some rare-earth materials, which are essentially superconductors. High energy electric pulses, maybe for a few milliseconds, are used to initiate the process within a fusion core.'

'Research shows that there can be two opposite reactions when using Palladium (Pd) as the core. We know that Pd isotopes have both capture and decay properties. So, choosing the right isotope is very important. At high temperatures, Pd^{103} captures an electron, merges with a proton, and forms a neutron in the process. This electron capture forms a new Rhodium (Rh^{103}) atom, and releases gamma ray of energetic photon. This reaction is of little use in energy production.'

'Another isotope of Palladium, Pd^{107}, becomes Silver atom (Ag^{107}), while releasing an electron through beta decay, as a proton is formed from a neutron. In the movie, a new element was generated in the procedure, which does not exist in the real world.'

'The gamma and beta rays generated from both the capture and decay procedures cannot be used as a source of energy, as they are compensated to balance the newly formed atomic nuclei. To harness energy of the electron from the beta decay process, we need to use both the isotopes of Palladium. Pd^{107} is used as an electron source for Pd^{103}, resulting in the creation of an electric circuit between the two isotopes. But, these two isotopes differ drastically in their radioactive nature. Pd^{107} is a stable isotope with a half-life of about 6.5 million years, while Pd^{103} is highly radioactive with a half-life of only 17 days. So, the inner ring of the electromagnet is made of Pd^{107}. A very small amount of Pd^{103} isotope, after being ionized by an electric arc, is made to rotate at high velocity within the outer ring, which can be made from Barium-Copper alloy.

They are both superconductors. While the tremendous kinetic energy generated from the high velocity of the isotope increases the chance of encountering a free electron, rapid ionization of the core can actually delay the process. Thus, the radioactivity of Pd^{103} can be controlled by simply manoeuvring the rate of ionization and the velocity of rotation within the ring.'

'Since the Tokamak is donut-shaped, the high-energy electrons from the Pd^{107} are directed towards the outer ring. The electrons are captured by the highly energized Pd^{103} ions, thus emitting gamma rays which are deflected by the outer magnetic ring to catalyse the beta decay of the inner ring. This deficit of electrons from the core creates a huge electrostatic potential in the inner ring, thus creating an electric cell with high voltage.'

'To start up the reaction, Pd^{103} is ionized by an external electric arc, and is made to rotate at high velocity using the superconductor magnetic ring. An electric current is generated within the Tokamak due to the potential difference between the inner and the outer ring. The gamma ray emission from Pd^{103} ions are deflected inwards to accelerate further emission of electrons from the inner core, and thus initiating a self-sustaining reaction. This slow reaction can further be accelerated by using a load for the flow of electric current generated.'

She referred to David Kirtley, Ph.D., who was the founder and CEO of Helion Energy, and described how he envisioned of building a practical model of fusion reactor on a commercial scale to generate electricity. It is speculated that he received a funding of $2.2 billion for his project.

Farah poured some water into a glass from the bottle kept on the table. Everyone was digesting the long and informative lecture she had delivered as a probable source of power for their upcoming prototype. If designed, this could be a breakthrough in the research for light-weight, self-sustaining and clean energy source. Everyone was really excited about the idea.

Adi spoke up, 'Now we need to think of creating a flight model for this.'

An Excursion

*S*hambhala was a place of serenity, a heavenly abode. It was a place where only the purest of souls could live, a place where love and wisdom reigned, and where the inhabitants were immune to all worldly desires and sufferings. Only individuals with appropriate Karma could reach there.

Agni took the bow away from Arjuna's hand, as per the protocol of the land, and led them towards the main entrance.

They were spellbound by the mesmerizing beauty of the city. They gaped at the striking admixture of natural elements with architectural feats as well as superior urban planning that surpassed Indraprastha by manifolds. Shambhala was indeed a dreamland, an illusion, about which every mortal being had imagined to be a part of.

The city was built in three tiers. Three different layers of Ashramas encircled the innermost administrative building.

The first Ashrama was the Gyanganj Math. People there were followers of the Sun and practised Surya Samadhi (solar worship). This was a place of great saints who had overcome their mundane dimensions and crossed over psychic barriers. Only highly enlightened saints could reach this place. This was also an extraordinary centre of spiritual training. The Brahmacharis, Brahmacharinis and Paramhansa Yogis of this place practised Surya Vigyan, Brahmavidya, Yoga, Tantra, Mantra, Science and Art and they influenced the world in subtle ways whenever needed. It was said that one could not get access to the Math unless they were predestined. Consciousness always remained alive in this enigmatic land as no death occurred there. One's journey did not end on reaching there. It was the beginning.... with the Endless.

Chapter Fourteen

THE MANOEUVRE

Anjan and Virat were experts in designing flight models. But this was special. They had to think of some avant-garde model which was in accordance with their project.

'Let's start from our school-day physics.' Virat was excited to begin the discussion. 'Let us suppose that, there is a metallic cylinder with a metallic ring around it. When electric current is flown through the cylindrical core, a magnetic field is set up. As a result of this magnetic field, a current is induced in the ring which sets up another magnetic field. As per Lenz's Law, these two magnetic fields thus produced have opposite polarities. In effect, the cylinder holds the ring around it, floating in air. The current in the core can be adjusted so that the ring can fly upwards, downwards, or can be suspended at a specific position in air relative to the core.'

An image flashed in Maya's head. Is that how the Sudarshan Chakra remained suspended around the finger of the Lord? Maybe, by His divine power, he could generate such a physical phenomenon simply by controlling the elements in His body!

Virat continued, 'The theory of using magnetic levitation in propulsion is not quite new. Many developed countries have started researching on it so that this can be used as a method of mass transit to avoid congestion created on surface transport system. Theoretically, three sets of magnetic loops are utilized in Maglev. One loop is used to suspend the system, controlling the vertical movement, while a second loop maintains the horizontal stability. Both these loops use the repulsive forces of electromagnets that are generated. The third loop utilizes both attraction and repulsion effect, by exploiting electromagnets that run on alternating electric current. If the transit system has north pole in the front and south pole at the back, the electromagnetic effect from the alternating current pulls it towards the front, as well as pushes it frontward from the back --- thus creating a forward motion. A strong field can create a transit speed as high as six hundred kmph. This is a very stable and safe system. The only factor to increase the efficiency is by using superconductors, which are however active at temperatures less than two hundred and thirty degrees below the normal freezing point of water.'

Anjan commented, 'A very simple practical use is demonstrated by Levitron toy. It is a simple magnetic top spinning on a magnetic base. The weight of the top and the levelling of the base balances the two vectors of magnetic repulsion and gravitational pull. Additionally, spinning momentum of the top balances the torque produced by any tilt of magnetic field, and further effect of gravity on it, thus providing stability. Too much or too little of this gyroscopic effect will again pull the top down.' Others were amused to know how he used an eraser or a pencil to balance the weight of such a top in his childhood days, and how many he lost while they flew off from the top.

'Using this simple physical phenomenon, a prototype of a flying machine can be built,' he continued. 'Two such electromagnetic plates when rotated in opposite directions, creates enough levitation force to hold it in the air. This can be a new technology for Unmanned Aerial Vehicles (UAV), which can further be developed to carry desired payloads as per requirement. If the initial torque can be generated by miniature portable fusion reactors, this will be an all-weather vehicle. As an alternative, to conserve the reaction, direct solar energy can be used for powering the levitation.'

It was clear that he was really inspired by each and every idea which they had discussed earlier, and the information which were revealed from the scriptures. This was actually bearing a resemblance to the spinning Chakra made up of powerful sun dust.

Further Revelations

The next tier was the Siddha Vigyan Ashrama. This was the scientific research centre for advanced Yoga. Sixteen forms of sciences were practised there, the most important being Surya Vigyan (Solar Science). Other forms included: Sarbajanina Graha Vigyan (Science of Universal Planetary system), Samaya Vigyan (Science of Time), Bayu Vigyana (Science of Air), Mahakasa Vigyan (Science of Space), Mahakarsiya Shakti Vigyan (Science of Gravity). All the sciences involved a high level of understanding of the Shakti, the feminine manifestation of the physical forces and energies available in nature. Each branch of Science had dedicated departments and laboratories, and the teachers present there were believed to be hundreds of years old, while some of them were as old as thousand years. People residing there worshipped the Parashakti, the ultimate energy of the universe, as their main deity.

The third and last was the Yoga Siddhashrama. The highest and supreme Yogis residing in this place believed only in the Governing Order of Divinity, which all others in the world referred to as GOD. They trained themselves to act as angelic beings so that they could exercise their knowledge and experience to maintain harmony in the Universe. In this way, these spiritual leaders intervened in the physical world through their subtle existence. It was possible to reach this land of Siddhas only if one had raised one's Kundalini Shakti from the Mooladhar or the Root Chakra.

This chakra is the lowest among the seven centres of human body which receives the energy of life from the cosmos through medulla oblongata. The highest among these is Saharsrara or the Crown Chakra. When all these centres are activated through meditation, an individual become free from the bondages of Shar…ripu (Kama, Krodha, Lobha, Moha, Mada and Matsarya), the six demonic senses and true enemies of a mortal life. In this state of life, one triumphs over this materialistic world and abandons every physical need of the existing body. This is and had always been the highest form of enlightenment. People believed that this was the place, the Paradise of Life, which every human being on earth had craved for eternity.

Chapter Fifteen

REAL LIFE JARVIS

Maya said with a thoughtful tone, 'Do you notice how JARVIS became Vision! After all, the MCU must have been inspired by the augmentation of the AI from a shapeless Generative Pre-trained Transformer (GPT) to the one with a form. Isn't it quite similar to the concept of Sudarshan? The scriptures repeatedly mentioned another aspect of the Chakra, probably humane. Even, Vision and Sudarshan sounds similar.'

She was referring to the Artificial Intelligence which was conceptualised in the Iron Man series of the Marvel franchise. It was the most obliging and loyal companion of the protagonist. According to the popular comic series, JARVIS got seriously damaged by the attacks of Ultron. Though the secret codes of the software continued to perform its task, in order to fully reinstate the system, Iron Man uploaded the core software in a physical body made of *vibranium*. An entirely new being was thus formed along with the use of an *Infinity Stone*, and he named it Vision.

Maya was excited as she was now plying in her own arena. She continued to describe how AI was transforming the world and the recent developments were pushing the limits of generative AI.

'Development of the new Auto-GPT is almost done. It is an open-source application, programmed in Python, and is a derivative of OpenAI's GPT-4. It is developed to function autonomously, has the ability to independently learn and adapt, and brings us closer to artificial general intelligence, without the need of the user to prompt for every action.'

She then elaborated the enhanced power of the AI to accomplish various tasks and projects. This marked the rise of AI agents which would bring about a major transformation in industrial revolution. This would create a whole new paradigm in the next phase and, is coined as Industry 4.0. This development would shape the future. The demonstrated prototype outperformed the much-hyped and recently popular ChatGPT with its state-of-the-art Natural Language Processing (NLP), with incredible capabilities of self-improvement.'

'If this can be combined with the highly advanced Lethal Autonomous Weapons System (LAWS), there will be no need of human intervention in any war. When implanted in the Atlas, the most advanced robot which can tread over any ground, clear any hindrance or even jump over an obstacle, it will change the course of future warfare altogether. The autonomous weapons system can even be incorporated in the robot dog Vision 60, which is capable of carrying a Kalashnikov and manoeuvre it autonomously.

Anjan started playing the Devil's advocate again. 'You are planning of integrating an enhanced AI in super precise robotics. There goes our future! Haven't you heard what Geoffrey Hinton, the father of AI, has said in a recent interview. He is now himself scared of the technology he has helped to build. He has even gone to the extent of opposing and organizing demonstrations against any further development of AI until human race clearly understands the purpose of this innovation.'

Virat nodded, as he quoted the famous statement by Albert Einstein, "I am not sure with which weapons the third world war will be fought but in the fourth world war they will fight with sticks and stones."

Maya ignored the interruptions from her team-mate as she continued, 'Research is going on to develop Evolutionary Cognitive Heuristic Operator, called ECHO. The debate between mankind and AI will be over after its successful launch. The difference between the human beings, with their awareness, cognition and consciousness, and AI, which are codes and programs without feelings, will be bridged forever. Combined with intelligence and conscience, this will make humankind redundant of any task like creating to-do lists, completing tasks, preparing podcasts, and developing web applications or any other programs. It will also be able to prepare research papers or articles based on given keywords and summarize existing research articles. In the military usage, this will not only decide how, when and whom to attack, but would apply its own logic to find out the reason behind an attack. It will also take necessary initiatives for offence and defence, build its own army as per the demand.'

'People are saying that this will be the end of mankind! They are scared. But I look at it from a different perspective. For centuries, mankind has been busy innovating things that will benefit them. It would allow them to live a hassle-free, peaceful life. Once AI takes over all such mundane requirements, people will then be free from all basic needs and will outdo all the levels of Maslow's pyramid. They will stop finding means of dominance and power, surpass the level of self-actualization, and delve deep to achieve the stage of transcendence. Don't we all dream of achieving this? Don't we all read it in our scriptures as that is the ultimate goal of human life? Don't we all envision this as the form of God?'

She reminded all with the famous quote of Lao Tzu, "In chaos there is fertility, and in destruction there is creation."

Sojourn

Draupadi was totally exhausted and could barely walk. On seeing her condition, Yudisthira decided to arrange her accommodation in the available quarters of the first tier of Shambhala. He also instructed two of his younger brothers, Sahadeva and Nakul to stay there to accompany her.

The trio, along with Agni, kept marching forward. There, they met the Chief Scientist and Head of all laboratories. He recognised them at once, and welcomed them with open arms.

Viswakarma ordered Agni to hand over the Gandiva Bow to Varuna, who was the Head of Weapons Department. Varuna was in charge of the safe-keeping of all the advanced weapons, which had already been used earlier in Wars, or were under research for future use.

Chapter Sixteen

THE BLUEPRINT

The next morning, the team assembled with rejoiced spirits. After a few days of explorations, discussions and brainstorming, it was time to plan and design the prototype of the subject for which they all gathered together.

The shape of the device was envisaged to represent two circular rotating discs. The design was most aerodynamic, as its shape would face minimum thrust, drag and air pressure. The flight would be controlled by magnetic levitation. The core of the device would be designed hollow. It would accommodate all the equipment for combat. At the centre, a Tokamak was planned to be fitted which would encase the miniature arc reactor. This would act as the source of power for the unmanned vehicle. Along with that, the core will have payloads of other telematic systems, sensors, processors and weaponry. The outer case would be devised with an alloy of tungsten and special aluminium, with minimum weight and high durability, while the inner core would be built with carbon fibre and diamond.

Inside the core, a complex bundle of sensors and processors would be set up. It would be loaded with highly advanced generative artificial intelligence, databases, with the ability of natural language processing and voice control. It would have features to latch on with the home-grown Indian Regional Navigation Satellite System, nicknamed NavIC. It would communicate with satellite-based edge computing system for the lowest latency, while using the diamond inside the core effectively for concentrating the signals travelling through the ionosphere with precision, acting as a booster. This would act as an alternative to the highly condensed array of antennas required for such communication, reducing complexity and achieving more precision with flexibility.

Advanced lock-on and lock-off systems would help to identify any target with highest meticulousness. While the payload would carry sophisticated long-range ballistic micro-missiles as a basic mode of weaponry, the main element in its arsenal would be directed energy weapons. Cutting-edge versions of miniaturized KALI and DURGA would be assembled within it.

Maya was drawing sketches in her notebook as per the feedbacks coming out of the discussions. Then she started giving the form of the prototype using a high-end digital editing software in her laptop. Each one of the team members provided valuable inputs for finalizing the prototype. When completed, they could not believe their eyes. The prototype thus developed was rotating and flying freely, communicating naturally on voice commands, and was emitting laser and gamma rays just like the very famous Chakra. This looked like a beautiful futuristic autonomous flying machine, which had the capability to strike with stealth, precision and power.

They then put their design on simulation. It was a perfect surreptitious flying machine. The spinning object was resembling the beautiful version of the celestial weapon while the emitting laser rays were symbolising the sunrays from which the mythical weapon was believed to be built. Voice commands in all major Indian languages were tested successfully. Also, they thought of incorporating the sensors capable of tuning in the five Gigahertz waves so that it communication could be directly established through the brain waves.

They were so happy that they decided to name their invention as if it was their own child. While the initial proposals were loosely based on the titles of their mission and the search and expedition for that, they finally zeroed in on a more generic label. This label would encompass all of their success, and would accommodate modifications, upon further research and developments.

It was named the ASTRA – an ingenuous acronym for AI-enabled Supersonic Tactical Reusable Armament.

Accomplishment

Viswakarma held out his hand and received the Box which Arjuna was still carrying. He said, 'This was my greatest invention of all time. I would secure it myself. Worry not, for it would be safeguarded and preserved here for centuries under optimal conditions. When time comes, I would personally hand it over to the rightful owner, the One who would emancipate the mankind upon his birth on this planet in the future. He would require His Dharohar to save humanity once again'. He also suggested Arjuna and Bheema to reside at the nearby quarters that encircled the Siddha Vigyan Ashramas, institutes of excellence for research in science and various allied technologies. He also asked them to share their lifelong experience and knowledge of winning numerous warfare, that ultimately created the path for establishing righteousness and peace.

Yudhisthira was now left all alone with the dog. He had already developed a familiar affection towards it. Both of them advanced to the last tier. Indra, the King of the Land, had sent a golden chariot to facilitate the rest of his journey. But, the gatekeepers persuaded him to abandon the dog, as they received an order to permit Yudhisthira only. Yudhisthira refused, and argued that his new pet also had the same rights to enter. This was a land of rectitude and equality, and every living soul in any form must be treated with dignity and honour. They had a prolonged debate. Pondering upon this delay, Indra himself arrived at the gates. He was abreast of all arguments and disagreements. He looked pleased, and approached Yudhisthira with a smile of satisfaction. He was happy to find that all these debates and negotiations had ultimately uphold the true persona of Yudhisthira, and he had attained the right to enter the Siddhashrama. Undoubtedly, he had proven himself to be the embodiment of morals, truth and virtues which he had established through his deeds in every act throughout his life, and was continuing till this last stage. He accompanied Yudhisthira to the grand court of the superiors. There, he was greeted by the Enlightened Ones who offered him to reside in the so-called Paradise of Life.

Chapter Seventeen

HOMECOMING

The team was in high spirits. They had successfully designed their prototype. While they sent the design to their headquarters (HQ) for expert suggestions and final approval, some scratches of incomplete drawings were left in the laptops. This was however against the standard protocol, as every trace of documentation and information should be deleted from all devices after sending them to HQ, especially during a coveted operation. But all of their devices were secured. It would be impossible to sneak in without destroying the hardware, as the encryption used in the devices were of the highest security levels.

It was time to return to their base and work further in order to give their design a physical shape, build an actual prototype for field testing, and delve into feasibility for production and development. They decided to travel by road to Jamnagar Airport, which was only a hundred and twenty-seven kilometres via NH947. This way they would get some extra time to spend together and rejuvenate, after mind-boggling saga of incidents they went through, over the last few days. As usual, Anjan took to the wheels.

By then, they had covered more than half of their journey, when Anjan noticed a black Audi trailing them through his rear-view mirror. The road had negligible traffic. The car which was following them suddenly sped vigorously towards them. Anjan was alarmed, he increased the speed of their car. Moments later, the Audi rammed into the car from behind and everyone inside jolted. Anjan was an efficient driver. He tried to manoeuvre the car and pressed the pedal to the floor. But it was a few seconds late. By that time the car from the back rammed again. This time he tried to swiftly turn to the right and then to the left in order to dodge the car. A service road was visible a few metres ahead. Though it was not a very good idea to take to the service road, and he was unsure where that road would lead to, he could not think of anything else at that moment. As he swerved his car to the service road, the car from behind kept chasing. But surprisingly, this time, the Audi was maintaining a constant distance, though close enough. The service road led to a lonely field with nothing in the vicinity. It was already getting dark. Though rattled at first, everyone knew that they had to find an escape route asap. They started searching for alternatives. Adi was unable to express anything as Anjan was at the wheels and he was trying to do whatever it was possible at that moment. Suddenly, a deafening sound shook them all, as a bullet hit the left rear wheel of their car. Anjan could not control the car, and it rolled off from the narrow road into the field beside. The car screeched to a halt, as it hit an electric pole at the side of the road. The front two airbags blew out, but the curtain window airbags did not blow as the car hit the pole at an angle. Everyone was wearing their seat belts, so there was no major injury to any of the passengers. They were in utter shock. Unable to move, they all remained seated within the car, and kept their doors locked.

The car chasing them also stopped a few metres away. All the doors opened, and four men came out of the car. Among them, three were carrying automatic light machine guns in their hands. The fourth one, visibly leading the team, was wearing a white shirt and blue denim, and held two small automatic pistols in both of his hands. He reached to their car followed by his henchmen. He knocked on the driver's window with his pistol, and ordered Anjan to come out of the car. Anjan opened the door, and got out of the car as there was no other option left. As he unlocked the door, the central lock inside the car got deactivated, and the three men with guns in their hands opened all the doors of the car. They ordered everyone to come out and form a line. They stood defenceless, with their hands raised up.

As Adi got out of the car, the leader of the gang held him from behind and pointed his gun at his head. Maya shook in a reflex of apprehension. He said in a voice filled with rage, 'You think, you can outsmart us? You stole our ideas, years of research and wasted our time and money. It was our dream project and we have invested more than you can imagine. You will hand over all your documents and blueprints immediately. Do not try to play any stupid game, rather, dare not think about it, or else we will open fire.

Give me all your belongings. Keep your cash and identity cards. We do not want any valuables too.' His eyes were shining at the prospect of retrieving the most precious thing he treasured. With a commanding tone, he ordered Adi to hand over the much coveted blueprint of the weapon. He directed the three others to search inside the car.

Maya was forced to bring out her laptop, which she handed over shakily to one of the members of the gang. The leader ordered all of them to submit their mobile phones too. They had no option but to comply before these heavily armed men. Then the leader said, pointing to Anjan, 'Your friend stays with us. Let's see if he can help us, and tell us the whole story. Don't worry, we will treat him as our guest.' He smiled creepily, and all of them approached the Audi parked nearby.

The four scientists were now sitting in the open field. Darkness consumed them both from outside and inside. They did not have any idea of their surroundings. Being unable to contact with anyone, they felt hopeless. Maya and Farah were deeply saddened at the fold of events and though they did not share much rapport with Anjan, they felt sorry for him. Exhausted and bewildered, the team surrendered themselves completely at the mercy of God. They could never imagine such an such an unpleasant ending to their incredible journey. It was quite late in the evening, as the crescent moon was about to set a little above the horizon, they could not do anything but sit and admire the night sky. They had no option to report anyone, seek any support or flee from there.

Over an hour or so passed by as they were left in the dark. Suddenly, they saw two dots of light in the distance. After a while, it was clear that those were the headlights of some approaching vehicles. A ray of hope gleamed before them, as they tried to shout out and seek the attention of the vehicles by waving their hands in anticipation. A police patrol van and an armoured vehicle following it stopped near them. One man in uniform came out of the van and said, 'Thank God you are here. It seems that they have left with whatever they were looking for, but I am relieved to see you unharmed. I am the Officer in Charge of the local Police Station. Our team is already deployed to investigate the incidents and nab the group behind the crime, after getting tip-off from some villagers who were the eye-witnesses to the whole episode from a distance. They however were not sure how to approach you, as they apprehended vengeance, hostility or retaliation from you. So, they informed us. Now, please follow me into my car. We will arrange a safe journey for you to the Jamnagar Airport. Our special forces will escort you. We have orders from the higher authority.' The team thanked him, and reached the local Police Station in the police van.

A white Jeep was waiting for them at the Police Station. A small convoy was arranged, with a pilot car and a security van. They reached the airport where a special chartered plane was waiting for them. The plane took off directly to their destination.

Back in Hyderabad, the Director was tracking every single move of the team. He was getting the exact locations of the team through the GPS enabled in their phones. He was concerned when their movement became still for a longer time than anticipated. He immediately rang the Home Ministry. It was a swift action, and officers from the Ministry and Intelligence Wing tracked down their last available location in co-ordination with the state police. The Director received a confirmatory call that the team had been rescued and were safe with the local police. He looked at his wrist watch to check the time. He took out his personal satellite phone and dialled a number. As he got a response from the other end, he conveyed in a firm voice, 'Sir, the ASTRA is exposed.'

Supplementary Readings and References

Research Papers

1. Arc reactor Technology: A Review: https://www.researchgate.net/publication/328161815_ Arc_reactor_Technology_A_Review
2. Levitron: Playing with Magnetic Levitation: http://web.mit.edu/viz/levitron/Physics.html
3. Simple theory for the Levitron: https://aip.scitation.org/doi/10.1063/1.365856#:~:text =A%20simple%20theory%20of%20its,various%20assu mptions%20for%20its%20orientation
4. Magnetic Levitation: https://www.encyclopedia.com/science-and-technology/physics/physics/magnetic-levitation
5. Magnetic Levitation: https://www.sciencedirect.com/topics/engineering/mag netic-levitation

Ebooks

1. The Story of Rudramahālaya: https://web.bookstruck.in/book/chapter/20340
2. Idols of Krishna: https://www.preserveculture.org/stories-gallery/3-idols-of-

krishna#:~:text=But%20Vajranabh%20was%20no%20o
rdinary,know%20how%20Krishna%20looked%20like

3. Attacks on the Jagannath Temple:
   https://medium.com/jai-jagannath/attacks-on-the-
   jagannath-temple-c401f4aea6bd

Online References

1. Aarsha Samskruti – Siddhashram:
   https://devoutnes.com/siddhashram-gyanganj/
2. Shambhala: https://en.wikipedia.org/wiki/Shambhala
3. Wikipedia – Vishvarupa:
   https://en.wikipedia.org/wiki/Vishvarupa
4. Government of Gujarat – Gir Somnath District:
   https://girsomnath.nic.in/history/#:~:text=Somnath's
   %20first%20temple%20is%20said,temple%20and%20de
   stroyed%20the%20temple
5. Somnath Temple:
   https://en.wikipedia.org/wiki/Somnath_temple
6. Issues and Challenges in India - Islamic Plunder of
   Somnath Temple:
   https://socialissuesindia.wordpress.com/islamic-
   plunder-of-somnath-temple/
7. Manat (goddess):
   https://en.wikipedia.org/wiki/Manat_(goddess)
8. Bhalka: https://en.wikipedia.org/wiki/Bhalka
9. Gujarat Tourism, Bhalka Teerth, Gir-Somnath:
   https://www.gujarattourism.com/saurashtra/gir-
   somnath/bhalka-tirth.html
10. Wikipedia–KALI (electron accelerator):
    https://en.m.wikipedia.org/wiki/KALI_(electron_acce
    lerator)
11. Wikipedia – Laser Weapon:
    https://en.m.wikipedia.org/wiki/Laser_weapon

12. Mahmud Ghaznavi: Why he attacked 17 times on India ?: https://www.jagranjosh.com/general-knowledge/mahmud-ghaznavi-why-he-attacked-17-times-on-india-1437387972-1

13. OLD SOMNATH TEMPLE (AHILYABAI HOLKAR TEMPLE): https://timesofindia.indiatimes.com/travel/Somnath/Old-Somnath-Temple-Ahilyabai-Holkar-Temple/ps47264048.cms

14. Dwarka: https://en.wikipedia.org/wiki/Dwarka

15. Akbarnama: https://en.wikipedia.org/wiki/Akbarnama

16. How Does Iron Man's Arc Reactor Work?: https://www.youtube.com/watch?v=ME1WdvuL6sE

17. How This Fusion Reactor Will Make Electricity by 2024: https://www.youtube.com/watch?v=4GJtGpvE1sQ

18. A material future for fusion?: https://www.chemistryworld.com/features/a-material-future-for-fusion/4015877.article

19. Do scriptures describe the effects of Brahmastra?: https://hinduism.stackexchange.com/questions/18961/do-scriptures-describe-the-effects-of-brahmastra

20. Mausala Parva: https://en.wikipedia.org/wiki/Mausala_Parva

21. How Ancient Astronaut Theorists Faked a Hindu Nuclear Explosion: https://www.jasoncolavito.com/the-case-of-the-false-quotes.html

22. Sudama: https://en.wikipedia.org/wiki/Sudama

23. Dvārakā: https://en.wikipedia.org/wiki/Dv%C4%81rak%C4%81

24. Bet Dwarka: https://en.wikipedia.org/wiki/Bet_Dwarka

25. Makaradhwaja:
https://en.wikipedia.org/wiki/Makaradhwaja
26. Archimedes:
https://en.wikipedia.org/wiki/Archimedes#Heat_ray
27. Directed-energy weapon:
https://en.wikipedia.org/wiki/Directed-energy_weapon
28. MIT Has Plans for a Real ARC Fusion Reactor > Iron Man's alma mater has a design for a realistic ARC fusion reactor: https://spectrum.ieee.org/mit-has-plans-for-a-real-arc-fusion-reactor
29. Indradyumna:
https://en.wikipedia.org/wiki/Indradyumna
30. Jagannath Temple, Puri:
https://en.wikipedia.org/wiki/Jagannath_Temple,_Puri#External_links
31. Jagannath:
https://en.wikipedia.org/wiki/Jagannath#Origins
32. Portal Gun and Magnetic Levitation:
https://www.wired.com/2012/10/hackadays-portal-gun-and-magnetic-levitation/
33. Coilgun: https://en.wikipedia.org/wiki/Coilgun
34. Magnetic Weapons:
https://tvtropes.org/pmwiki/pmwiki.php/Main/MagneticWeapons
35. Magnetic Levitation:
https://en.wikipedia.org/wiki/Magnetic_levitation
36. Maglev: https://en.wikipedia.org/wiki/Maglev
37. The Legend and Destruction of Martand, The Sun Temple in Kashmir: https://www.sanskritimagazine.com/the-legend-and-destruction-of-martand-the-sun-temple-in-kashmir/
38. Martand Sun Temple:
https://en.wikipedia.org/wiki/Martand_Sun_Temple

39. Sun Temple, Modhera: https://en.wikipedia.org/wiki/Sun_Temple,_Modhera
40. Ayodhya Dispute: https://en.wikipedia.org/wiki/Ayodhya_dispute
41. Ram Mandir: https://en.wikipedia.org/wiki/Ram_Mandir
42. Gyanvapi Mosque: https://en.wikipedia.org/wiki/Gyanvapi_Mosque
43. Krishna Janmasthan Temple Complex: https://en.wikipedia.org/wiki/Krishna_Janmasthan_Temple_Complex#References
44. Krishna Janmabhoomi – An Ignored Chapter Of Perseverance In Indian History: https://pragyata.com/krishna-janmabhoomi-an-ignored-chapter-of-perseverance-in-indian-history/
45. Hampi: https://en.wikipedia.org/wiki/Hampi
46. Mythology of Hampi: https://hampi.in/mythology-of-hampi
47. Siddhpur: https://en.wikipedia.org/wiki/Siddhpur
48. Rudra Mahalaya Temple: https://en.wikiquote.org/wiki/Rudra_Mahalaya_Temple
49. Radha Madan Mohan Temple, Vrindavan: https://en.wikipedia.org/wiki/Radha_Madan_Mohan_Temple,_Vrindavan
50. Madan Mohan Temple: https://en.wikipedia.org/wiki/Madan_Mohan_Temple
51. Holy Dham: https://www.holydham.com/sri-sri-radha-madana-mohana-temple/
52. Sri Radha Madan Mohan Temple Vrindavan: https://www.tourmyindia.com/states/uttarpradesh/sri-radha-madan-mohan-temple-vrindavan.html
53. Vajra: https://www.jatland.com/home/Vajra
54. Chaitanya Mahaprabhu: https://en.wikipedia.org/wiki/Chaitanya_Mahaprabhu

55. Nabakalebara 2015: https://en.wikipedia.org/wiki/Nabakalebara_2015

56. Maa Mangala Temple, Kakatpur: https://en.wikipedia.org/wiki/Maa_Mangala_Temple,_Kakatpur

57. Hindu Responses to Islamic Invasions: A Historical Journey: https://www.dharmadispatch.in/history/hindu-responses-to-islamic-invasions-a-historical-journey

58. Muslim conquests in the Indian subcontinent: https://en.wikipedia.org/wiki/Muslim_conquests_in_the_Indian_subcontinent

59. J.A.R.V.I.S.: https://en.wikipedia.org/wiki/J.A.R.V.I.S

60. Islamic Destruction of Hindu Temples: https://www.stephen-knapp.com/islamic_destruction_of_hindu_temples.htm

61. 10 Hindu Temples Destroyed by Muslim Rulers in India: https://vedicfeed.com/hindu-temples-destroyed-by-muslim/

62. Invasions on the Temple of Lord Jagannath, Puri: https://magazines.odisha.gov.in/Orissareview/2011/july/engpdf/82-89.pdf

63. AutoGPT: the real-life Jarvis AI from Iron Man?: https://www.verdict.co.uk/autogpt-generative-ai/#catfish

64. AUTOGPT: https://autogpt.net/category/chatgpt-tools/autogpt/page/2/

News Articles

1. Ancient Origins – Mysteries of the Kingdom of Shambhala (5 April, 2014): https://www.ancient-

origins.net/ancient-places-asia/mysteries-kingdom-shambhala-001529

2. Indiapost – Somanth : Looted, destroyed and resurrected 17 times (July 6, 2012): https://www.indiapost.com/somnath-looted-destroyed-and-resurrected-17-times/

3. Books Fact - Somnath to Antarctica, straight line without land (Sep 17, 2016): https://www.booksfact.com/history/somnath-antarctica-straight-line-without-land.html

4. Newbust (Dec 29, 2020): https://newsbust.in/archaeological-department-revealed-there-is-also-a-three-storey-building-under-the-somnath-temple-under-the-somnath-temple-is-a-3-storey-building-and-buddhist-caves-examined-up-to-12-meters-ins/

5. News TV Facebook page - The most dreaded weapons of 2023 ready (Sep 7, 2022): https://www.facebook.com/watch/?v=854198935939358&extid=WA-UNK-UNK-UNK-AN_GK0T-GK1C&ref=sharing

6. The Week – DRDO developing DURGA II laser weapon for land, naval, air use? (March 17, 2021): https://www.theweek.in/news/sci-tech/2021/03/17/drdo-developing-durga-ii-laser-weapon-for-land-naval-air-use.html

7. Ghazni to Brutal Aurangzeb, many attacks made but glory of 'Somnath Temple' did not diminish – by News Track, Aug 20, 2021: https://english.newstracklive.com/news/history-of-somnath-temple-how-many-times-invaders-razed-it-and-hindu-kings-raised-it-mc23-nu764-ta764-ta321-1177808-1.html

8. Why was Somnath temple destroyed 17 times? – Myfauth.com, December 7, 2021:

https://myfayth.com/hindusim/why-was-somnath-temple-destroyed-17-times/

9. How Maglev Works: https://www.energy.gov/articles/how-maglev-works#:~:text=The%20front%20corners%20have%20magnets,design%20creates%20a%20smooth%20trip

10. Gyanvapi Complex: History Of Kashi Vishwanath Temple, Its Present And Future: https://www.outlookindia.com/magazine/national/gyanvapi-complex-history-of-kashi-vishwanath-temple-its-present-and-future-magazine-198538

11. Kashi Vishwanath temple was built and demolished 3 times – the known and unknown history: https://www.timesnownews.com/opinion/kashi-vishwanath-temple-was-built-and-demolished-3-times-the-known-and-unknown-history-article-91616334#:~:text=Anecdotal%20history%20has%20it%20that,temple%20and%20the%20Gyanvapi%20mosque

12. Beyond the Hindu-Muslim binary: https://frontline.thehindu.com/arts-and-culture/heritage/beyond-the-hindu-muslim-binary/article25880107.ece

13. The Fascinating History and Story of Hampi And Vijayanagara Empire: https://www.india.com/travel/articles/the-fascinating-history-and-story-of-hampi-and-vijayanagara-empire-3231767/

14. Brahma Padartha: The Unsolved Mystery Of Nabakalebara: https://sambadenglish.com/brahma-padartha-the-unsolved-mystery-of-nabakalebara/

15. When Mahmud Ghaznavi attacked Somnath Temple on this day – Here is what happened: https://organiser.org/2023/01/08/103793/bharat/wh

en-mahmud-ghaznavi-attacked-somnath-temple-on-this-day-here-is-what-happened/

16. India's Hindu Right Is Correct About One Thing: India's Muslim Rulers Did Destroy Hindu Temples: https://thediplomat.com/2016/08/indias-hindu-right-is-correct-about-one-thing-indias-muslim-rulers-did-destroy-hindu-temples/

Blog Articles

1. What is Gyanganj and where is it: https://www.quora.com/What-is-Gyanganj-and-where-is-it

2. In the Mahabharata how many times Brahmastra was used from beginning to end?: https://www.quora.com/In-the-Mahabharata-how-many-times-Brahmastra-was-used-from-beginning-to-end

3. What happened with Indraprastha, a capital of Pandavas in Mahabharata, when Pandavas won the great war, and capture a throne of Hastinapur?: https://www.quora.com/What-happened-with-Indraprastha-a-capital-of-Pandavas-in-Mahabharata-when-Pandavas-won-the-great-war-and-capture-a-throne-of-Hastinapur

4. Magnet Cannon: https://www.kjmagnetics.com/blog.asp?p=magnet-cannon

5. Electromagnetic Levitation: https://www.kjmagnetics.com/blog.asp?p=electromagnetic-levitation

6. Magnetic Levitation: How Maglev Works: https://scitechdaily.com/magnetic-levitation-how-maglev-works/

7. Stories in Stone at the Sun temple of Modhera | A guide on Modhera Sun Temple Gujarat: https://thrillingtravel.in/sun-temple-of-modhera-gujarat.html

8. The story of how Kashi Vishwanath Temple was destroyed, restored and finally re-established: https://tfipost.com/2021/12/the-story-of-how-kashi-vishwanath-mandir-was-destroyed-restored-and-finally-re-established/

9. How Krishna Janmabhoomi Was Destroyed By Aurangzeb: https://kreately.in/aurangzeb-the-pious-destroyer-of-keshava-temple-in-mathura-his-possible-remorse/

10. Hampi chronicles: The curse that saved a temple: https://milesandsmiles.net.in/2021/02/04/hampi-chronicles-it-is-a-tale-of-two-brothers-a-sacred-geography-and-one-legendary-sage%e2%9a%94%ef%b8%8f/

11. Why is Hampi Called the City of Ruins?: https://www.thrillophilia.com/questions/why-is-hampi-called-the-city-of-ruins

12. Siddhpur, a Matru-Shradh pace in Gujarat: https://magikindia.com/siddhpur-gujarat/

13. My India My Glory: https://www.myindiamyglory.com/2018/04/09/rudra-mahalaya-a-10th-century-siva-temple-awaiting-revival-of-worship/

14. Struggle for Hindu Existence: https://hinduexistence.org/2016/11/24/how-a-hindu-symbol-of-solanki-dynasty-turned-into-mosque/

15. What is a list of Hindu temples destroyed by Islamic invaders?: https://www.quora.com/What-is-a-list-of-Hindu-temples-destroyed-by-Islamic-invaders

16. Why did Muslim invaders and rulers destroy Indian temples and other historical places?:

https://www.quora.com/Why-did-Muslim-invaders-and-rulers-destroy-Indian-temples-and-other-historical-places

17. Who were the top 5 Muslim invaders of India?: https://www.quora.com/Who-were-the-top-5-Muslim-invaders-of-India

18. How could the Islamic invaders not destroy Puri Jagannath Temple?: https://www.quora.com/How-could-the-Islamic-invaders-not-destroy-Puri-Jagannath-Temple

19. A Brief List of the Destruction of Temple s in Ancient India: https://www.patheos.com/blogs/hindu2/2018/11/a-brief-list-of-the-destruction-of-temples-in-ancient-india/

20. Jagannath Puri: Survivor of 18 invasions: https://indiafacts.org/jagannath-puri-survivor-18-invasions/

21. What is AutoGPT and how can I benefit from it?: https://lablab.ai/blog/what-is-autogpt-and-how-can-i-benefit-from-it

22. Maslow's Hierarchy of Needs for Motivation: https://www.communicationtheory.org/maslows-hierarchy-of-needs/

Social Media :

1. Praveen Mohan Facebook page – Ancient Gods in India (August 5, 2020): https://www.facebook.com/watch/?extid=WA-UNK-UNK-UNK-AN_GK0T-GK1C&v=1318049968403891

2. Secrets of ancient India - Siddhashram Gyanganj (The Abode of Immortal Masters): https://m.facebook.com/HiddenSecretsOfAncientIndia

/photos/siddhashram-gyanganj-the-abode-of-immortal-masters-this-universe-is-a-boundless-/434011046743880/

Video Resources

1. Youtube - Strange History of Chakra / Chakram - Ancient Weapon of India, by Praveen Mohan (Jan 30, 2019): https://www.youtube.com/watch?v=QInUkELKlBc
2. Strange History of Chakra / Chakram - Ancient Weapon of India: https://www.youtube.com/watch?v=QInUkELKlBcPreface
3. The lost city of dwarka | The city of lord Krishna: https://www.youtube.com/watch?v=eFAxM1gO7N0
4. EP 10 Shri Dwarka Dham Temple visit, Khichdi Osaman and market visit, visa2explore: https://www.youtube.com/watch?v=uz8ww5fhbyI
5. EP 11 Beyt Dwarka, Shree Dwarka temple, Shivrajpur beach | Gujarat Tourism: https://www.youtube.com/watch?v=uVY1tv3Kppk
6. Ancient Underground Tunnels found in India - Path to 'Paatal Lok' Revealed: https://youtu.be/iQF6YGpuRdE

Picture Sources

Wikepedia

List of **DRDO** Centres Mentioned

In The Story

1. Advanced Numerical Research & Analysis Group (ANURAG) – Hyderabad - Computational System
2. Advanced Systems Laboratory (ASL) – Hyderabad - Missiles & Strategic Systems
3. Centre for High Energy Systems and Sciences (CHESS) – Hyderabad – High Energy Weapons
4. Defence Research & Development Laboratory (DRDL) – Hyderabad – Missile and Strategic Systems
5. Research Centre Imarat (RCI) – Hyderabad - Missile and Strategic Systems
6. Advanced Centre for Research in High Energy Materials (ACRHEM) – Hyderabad – High Energy Materials
7. Centre for Advanced Systems (CAS) – Hyderabad – Advanced Systems
8. Aeronautical Development Establishment (ADE) – Bengaluru – Aeronautics
9. Centre for Air Borne System (CABS) – Bengaluru - Air Borne System (CABS)
10. Defence Avionics Research Establishment (DARE) – Bengaluru – Avionics